Copyright © 2023 Andrew

All rights reserved

Cover design by: Megan Bednarczyk
Printed in the United States of America

CONTENTS

The Creative Team

Notes On Organization And Leadership For The Business Of Creativity

FORWARD

I grew up professionally in a strange time for Advertising. Like a lot of industries nuked by the internet, advertising went through a period of wrenching change where the skills and values honed in the previous decades teetered and fell as they lost value. As the industry evolved and the people in it struggled to, there were many opportunities for digital minded creatives to advance their career. I was well positioned and well supported to do so. And so I did.

But as I found myself leading ever larger teams and projects, I could feel that I was getting over my skis. I was managing people older than myself on teams with skill sets I didn't have in an organization I didn't understand. If I think enough about this now I could still have a stress dream about it.

Looking for more solid footing, I read a lot - everything from business classics like Good to Great to creative ones like Creativity Inc. But what I found in business books was more about celebrating the story of giant successful companies than the small-ball daily details of building a successful team. I also noticed that when I asked for advice from friends and colleagues, what I got was more likely to be a sports reference or chef's quote than something from The One Minute Manager - the only management book ever handed out as training by any of my various employers.

If there is a catalog of the tactical know how and strategic questions of leading a creative team, I never did find it. This book is my take at writing it.

This is not a how-to on design or campaigns that impact culture. Neither is it a book on the creative process, inspiring teams or excellence. There is so much good writing from brilliant people in the world already, consuming only the best works on design, advertising, software and creativity could take years.

Instead, this is a book about operations and organization. It's about the peculiar mix of dynamics in a misunderstood corner of the corporate world; the creative team. It is my attempt to organize and summarize the learned and earned lessons of my journey from managing my first creative team of three, to the role of Chief Creative Officer with a multi-office, multi-discipline remit. It is about the many things beyond the work that come with creative leadership. It is peculiar to my own experience, leading digital focused teams in the New York based advertising culture in the 2000's but I suspect a lot of it would be relevant in any creative leadership role.

What follows are all the things I wish someone had told me when I stopped being responsible for the work alone, and started being responsible for everything else.

WHEN IT'S WORKING

It came in the way these things do sometimes in an advertising holding company. The brief was an ecommerce project for TJMaxx.com that had been kicking around between different agencies for weeks while they vetted the size of the opportunity (small) and whether they could manage any conflicts (no). By the time it hit my inbox, the pitch itself was two days away, in-person in Boston, and the New Business lead was a little sheepish about even bringing it up. It was late in the fiscal year. Every little bit of revenue was another win in the forecast. We would have one working day before I had to travel to deliver the presentation.

Could we do it?

New business pitches are always a crucible. There is never enough time, always too much to do and their competitive nature makes whatever you produce for them a little more stark. At the end of most presentations you have some feedback and some happy stakeholders. At the end of a new business pitch you either win or lose. They are clarifying that way.

Staffing wasn't an issue - a team had just wrapped work on another client and hadn't been reassigned yet. Six rested creatives without much to do. Six creatives who had worked together for years - some of us nearly a decade. Three of them former interns who had only ever worked at this company, and with this team. I skipped through the brief with my leads taking notes and talking through answers. One of them pulled inspiration designs while we talked. The other sketched in the margins of the brief and flipped through the site we were meant to re-think, pointing out problems.

We could do it.

We kicked off as a team at ten the next morning. When I told the team what we were doing, there wasn't any grousing or complaining - far from it. They laughed. Laughed and asked for the brief. Someone joked that I was trying to make other teams feel bad. We were fast, we knew it and we were borderline arrogant about it.

We started the way we usually did. Flipping through what the clients had shared, working out how to describe what they should be doing, sketching and ideating, hanging work and googling. Making fun of one another and trying to decide what to order for lunch. Since I would be giving the presentation, I wrote the narrative, and kept hanging new parts of it on the wall by our shared desk as I worked them out. Different designers picked off pages to elaborate. Someone passed a grid around. Someone else a sheet of type styles and later one of color hex values. Sketches, designs, key-frame copy and features all appeared on the wall and in the deck, were combined, cut, and shaped. Slack was a nonstop stream of files passing back and forth. Someone would shout that they needed a line or a design solution and someone else would run over to their monitor and work through it. There were so many asks, ideas and executions flying around that it would be hard to say how we were working. There were no recognizable meetings, activities or formal reviews. In their place, a strange creative choreography. A professional blur.

At eight that night we were pencils down. The deck was about thirty slides of work - not including cases and credentials - and included designs for all the problem pages, some with nice animation touches. It painted a vision of a far better, more creative, high-touch version of the TJMaxx site, wrapped in a compelling change story. All done during the course of pretty typical New York business hours.

When we got word that we'd won, I remember a lot of surprise in the agency but none on my team. No surprise but plenty of pride. This is how we did it. We expected good things to follow. The pitch itself had been less stressful than the early morning Delta shuttle out of LaGuardia. Good work presents itself. According to our future clients, there were six agencies in the pitch and it hadn't been close. Our ideas were better. Designs sharper. Writing more on-brand. Thinking clearer. Against a massive time deficit, we won on quality of creativity.

WHEN IT'S BROKEN

There are too many people.

Whatever else is happening, there are too many people for this brief so now none of them knows what to do. Is it a shootout? Are we doing this together? How are we choosing a direction? Who is? Nobody says. There isn't a creative leader, there are senior people who won't produce anything, will review work and give feedback, and might share the work with their boss or cut it. Might not. No one says. Some of the senior people who won't do anything are here now, and others who will "want to see this" will be in later meetings. The strategist doing the briefing mentions this unhelpfully.

The kickoff is standing room only. A lot of the faces are unfamiliar. There are no introductions. Some of the creatives on hand are listening while others read ahead or play with their phones. Time stops. Apart from the strategist, the room is dead quiet and broom clean. It could be any conference room in any company anywhere on corporate planet Earth. It will stay that way throughout the project.

Everyone has been in this meeting before. This group project. This freshman weeder course. So many nameless people. Someone has a question. The strategist is happy for it but in the back you can hear someone sigh and slap their notebook back down on the table. Why isn't this over yet? The woman with the question is new. She gives a sheepish apology if this isn't the right time to ask this. She hasn't learned not to speak.

There are no more questions. No ideas. No conversation or speech of any kind. All these people at a wake. A real wake would be more fun. It could have been an email and some of those present are thinking so. When it ends the creatives wander off in ones and twos, passengers deplaning, tired of confinement and each other. A mob dispersing.

The isolation is relief. The awkwardness is over and won't be back until someone schedules a formal internal review. Some of the pairs will catch up with some of the senior creatives who aren't making anything. They are the favorites and they work in cliques. The others are miscast, underskilled or both. They are here because they had free time. A staffing functionary wanted to get them busy. Scientific management and interchangeable creative cogs. Now they're all here in the hope that enough of the wrong people could make a right one. The wrong people know their work won't be picked, even if somehow they pull through and nail the brief. At best they will be expensive production for one of the cliques later on. For now everyone pretends otherwise.

The cliques will get around to finishing the brief and then find their own entertainment. The miscast will spend weeks doing the wrong thing and won't be told that's what they did, even in what passes for a review. They might present their work but more likely will email it into the digital void where it will be professionally ghosted.

And then they wait. The black box is processing. The creatives will wait until they are told they can leave. They are not told. Changes trickle in. Sometimes in emails or short directives. Dinner is ordered. Decision makers do drive bys. They are unhurried. A few of those earlier comments no longer apply. Change it back. Anyone could make these changes. The decision makers could. They don't. Some of the cliques have gone home for the night but the decision makers seem not to notice. The creatives who have stayed make more updates.

When the last of the decision makers leaves to meet some friends that are out, they cut the creatives loose. Weekend plans are canceled and check-ins are added. The ones who resist are scolded. Raised eyebrows. Parental disapproval.

This is what it takes to be great.

PROBLEMS

THE INHERITANCE PROBLEM

"The essence of strategy is choosing what not to do."

- MICHAEL PORTER

What do you want this team to be?

Unless you are an entrepreneur inventing something from scratch, this is an easy question to overlook. Most of us become creative leaders through rounds of promotion, attrition, luck and skill. We grew up or were hired-into structures and teams that existed before we arrived. Leaders led, we learned. We did it their way even when we hated it, and we got good enough at their way to excel at it. We took part in the traditions. Got the reviews, gave the presentations and worked through the feedback. We came in and went home and talked and walked and otherwise acted in line with the norms that were there when we got there.

And then we got promoted.

We inherited a thing. Some sort of creative team or department. And we were asked to shape and lead it.

If by good fortune, you have found yourself in this situation please consider this:
You do not have to accept anything about the team as given. Not the people or the practices, not the training or the structure. Not the tools or the deliverables. Not the view of what good work looks like or even the kind of good work you want to be doing.

You don't have to accept any of it. You can make it yours.

But to do that, you are going to have to articulate what you want it to be. You have to think about it. You have to decide. You have to be able to say it's this and not that and here's why. And you are going to have to share it as many ways as you can possibly think of, because if you don't, instead of you deciding it will just happen.

I propose to you that 'it just happened' is not what this promotion is about. 'It just happened' is an abdication. It's the worst possible use of the opportunity ahead. 'It just happened' isn't a vision. It's not a movement that people can get behind. 'It just happened' might not happen the way you want, might not happen at all, and then what?

This is your moment.

You inherited this thing and now you are about to happen to everyone and everything in the team you are leading. What will that be? Time you did some deciding.

THE SCALE PROBLEM

"Cooks who are really good at cooking almost always make horrible chefs."

- DAVID CHANG

You got this job because, whether you can explain it or not, you produced a certain kind of outcome on a certain kind of assignment. You were the one sharpening the points and filing down the extra bits. You were probably the one out front, explaining and advocating when the people with leadership titles weren't around. You got here on a team that had direct access to you. As part of your little team, you were policing the work and pushing the quality. You were communicating with all the makers all the time because you're a maker yourself. You were deep in the creative part of the creating and that showed in the work.

That got you promoted to leadership. And that isn't going to work anymore.

The most base problem with scaling creativity is the problem of getting beyond you. There isn't enough of you to go around. There aren't enough projects, flights, coffees or work sessions to shape your team through action. You can't animate the prototype. You can't write the script.

The work is still your problem, but creating just became the wrong way to solve it.

This problem is at the heart of management. How does one person, limited by time and geography, impact the work of many people and the outcomes of many assignments?
This is the scale problem.

I suspect that the scale problem is worse for creatives. The ephemeral nature of the work tends to defy processes and easy explanation. The phenomenon of a team producing nothing tangible for literal weeks, before creating a world beating idea in a few hours is a real one. So much of the work is thinking, talking, reading, searching, exploring and editing. It doesn't feel like productive work the way so many other jobs do where a steady accumulation of progress reaches a predictable conclusion. Creative work is less stepwise evolution and more punctuated equilibrium. To outsiders used to presenting tidy, linear processes the sausage making is a terror. Great creatives get comfortable with it. Thrive in it.

And then they become managers. The scale problem manifests itself in not-doing. A designer, whose sublime expression of type and color leads to promotion, is told to not-design (or design less). A writer, promoted for their big idea authorship and ease of producing elegant turns of phrase must not-write (or write less). The most basic assumption of management is scale. Unsaid in your promotion is the desire that you apply all the good attributes of your own craft skill onto the work of others. By asking you to lead, your boss is asking you to share the alchemy of your creativity. The assumption is that your own not-doing will confer your abilities to your team, making the whole better.

This is pretty tenuous stuff. Experts are notoriously bad at explaining their area of expertise. Organizational Psychologist

Adam Grant could have been describing an ECD when he said about his Harvard professors, "It wasn't that they didn't care about teaching. It was that they knew too much about their subject, and had mastered it too long ago, to relate to my ignorance about it."

Being a great generator of work is not the same skill as being a great integrator or editor of it. And now, leading a team, that is exactly what creative scale requires.

Charged with leading a team, but lacking many needed skills to do so, creative leaders fall back on what got them promoted in the first place. They become an expensive creative doer. They use the members of their team as "hands" to extend their own abilities and micromanage every aspect of the work. They have the idea. They author the execution. The hands stop thinking and make artifacts.

You can survive this way for a while. With only a couple of projects, or a small team, using your team for hands is a short term fix for scale. The flaws begin showing when you try to scale up and you can't be everywhere. Team members used to being cogs don't have the executive skills to have their own ideas or self-edit work when you aren't there to do it for them. They spin and they wait for direction, just like you taught them. Stretched beyond your ability to contribute, you can't create work fast enough for others to execute it. Time, the ultimate limiting factor on creativity, asserts its control. Projects collapse. You stop producing the kind of work that got you promoted.

Scale is a leadership problem. It is the muscle you will have to build to stay in your shiny new leadership job.

THE SKILL PROBLEM

"*The Dunning-Kruger effect, in psychology, is a cognitive bias whereby people with limited knowledge or competence in a given intellectual or social domain greatly overestimate their own knowledge or competence in that domain relative to objective criteria or to the performance of their peers or of people in general.*"

— ENCYCLOPEDIA BRITANNICA

"*At Christmas, everyone thinks they're Martha Stewart.*"

— UNKNOWN

I n most professions, early promotions mean leading others with the same craft skills as your own. Programmers are promoted to lead teams of programmers, consultants over teams of consultants, chefs over line cooks, on and on. Eventually, promotions mean leading people with adjacent or completely different skills from your own.

In creative professions, the range of craft skills causes this to happen sooner. It is the norm for the lowest level of creative managers to lead teams with writers, designers, art directors, editors, user experience professionals and others. The math of team composition says the odds are good that more of your team than not comes from a different discipline than yourself. This will be a source of immense frustration for you and for them.

Whereas you have a deep, detailed understanding of your own craft, quality, dirty tricks and sucker punches, you probably don't have more than a surface understanding of the ones adjacent to you. You know enough to know if something is good, but not enough to be directive about making it better. You will have a sense of what you want. You will definitely know it when you see it. But you don't have the vernacular or technique to get someone from where they are, to where you want them by giving feedback. This can feel like running in sand, and lead you to being more directive.

And then you step in the skill problem. Flush with the pride and achievement of an earned leadership role, too many creatives overestimate what they have to contribute to adjacent craft skills. Feeling their promotion, they start giving explicit direction when they should be asking for advice. Instead of owning the conceptual goal posts, they rewrite the headlines (Designers are insulated somewhat by their tools. Everyone thinks they can write). This is a career growth moment. Instead of faking your way through craft feedback, you should be relying on the best team member you can find in every craft other than your own. Instead of giving direction, you should be challenging and listening.

This will go against what you think is expected of you in leadership. It means mastering communication in places you used to rely on skill. Trusting others to work through their creative process. Patience, dialogue and the humility to admit you don't have the answer to this problem but you are here to help support your team as they find it.

FOUNDATION

CHANGE THE
DEFAULT SETTINGS

"Too often we find comfort in what worked before, even when it stops working."

\- BILL WALSH

Unless you are starting a brand new team or department from scratch (fun!) every avenue for shaping it has a default setting. Your recruiters target a set of schools or professional sites they are familiar with. Your creatives sit in a certain arrangement, working away with a set of tools on a set of deliverables using some sort of process. And you didn't choose any of it.

Default settings tend to have an oral history around why they are what they are. We recruit Brown because a past exec was an alumni. We use inDesign for presentations because three years ago our senior most Art Director switched us to it and procurement keeps renewing the license. We get cupcakes from the bakery around the corner on birthdays because....that's what we do? That's what we have always done.

You may not want to pay attention to these things. Choosing to is a time commitment you might feel you can't afford. Switching to a new tool stack is a shortcut to an inbox full of complaints. New processes raise eyebrows. Even if people don't like where they sit, they will grumble about having to move. Change - even change for the better - has a cost.

So why change?
Because defaults scale.

Defaults let you control quality when you aren't in the room. Defaults shape the team and the output without pushing pixels or re-writing copy. If you keep the defaults, you are letting whoever had the job before you (or before them) decide on your behalf. I hope you liked their vision, because now, in some way, you're executing it. You're giving up the chance to shape all the things that shape the work. You're settling for some part of someone else's version of what this should be. Maybe that's fine. Maybe they made good choices, and you only have to be a caretaker for your team to succeed. But if you don't re-examine the defaults, you won't ever be sure.

That's why it's so important to spend the energy - and it is a lot of energy - to reexamine your team's defaults and change the ones that don't support your vision. Defaults are lasting and structural. They impact culture and quality. A great team concept can fail because distant decisions about key controls are trundling along like zombies in the work culture.

You don't have to change them all at once. You're like a coach installing a new offense. It's going to take time. Start with the ones that feel out of date. That run counter to what you want to be. These could be anything, but the following are the most common I have encountered on creative teams.

Default Artifacts

Creatives can have a false economy about deliverables. If you can charge a client for a thing or show it to a stakeholder as proof of work, that thing proliferates and takes on an exaggerated importance. Its reason for being is divorced from quality or communication and boiled down to "because they pay us." or "because he likes it." Over the years, I have found and killed biblical specifications that no developer read, robust taxonomies that never informed a site design and criminal profile-worthy personas that creative teams shrugged at before tossing aside. That most of the default artifacts came from the UX discipline (my own early background) made it all the more frustrating.

Unused artifacts are the illusion of work. Every one that doesn't inform output seen by a customer is a block of time misallocated. Artifact making skill sets (technical writing, presentation design, etc) tend not to have much transfer to actual creativity. It only takes a few useless creative artifacts to distort your entire department into a pseudo management consultancy.

Because they tend to be inputs into other work, you can spot a zombie artifact by asking who it's for and then asking the intended audience how much it improves their work quality. Good artifacts, like customer journeys or briefs are force multipliers that save teams days or weeks of independent discovery. Bad artifacts do not.

If you are unsure which you inherited, let the intended audience decide. If the spec is for developers who don't read it, if the persona is for designers who don't find it unlocks better solutions, it's a time sink default, and you should change it.

Default Process

Why are you having that internal review? Why are there so many people in the kickoff and why are all the kickoffs one hour long? Why does everyone go back to their own desk to work alone afterwards? Why are our brainstorms always a bunch of people free-forming around a table? Why isn't anyone writing anything down? Why am I asking about this?

Many creatives are allergic to processes. Attempts at formalized rigor sound like paint by number self-help solutions to what we understand is an intangible thing. There is no big idea in six easy steps, and we're fine with that.

Yet for all the (mostly) correct skepticism we have about all things process, we are sheep to the slaughter in our acceptance of inherited ways of working. The most punk rock, bomb throwing Creative Directors show up with print outs to an internal review for the Account team two days after kickoff without so much as a peep about why we're having it at all.

This is too bad. The way we work can unleash the capability of everyone on the team. The right amount of the right process covers up for everyone's worst tendencies and puts them into a position where they are more likely to succeed. The wrong processes do the opposite. Time spent preparing presentation materials for an unneeded review is time that could have been spent on work. Presenting to a peer as though they were a client creates a power dynamic that is neither helpful or deserved. Unstructured brainstorms produce inferior outcomes.

As a creative leader, these may be the least appealing defaults to deal with. The creatives on your team will chafe at any formal "right" way of doing things. Other capabilities will fight any change in an approach optimized for their own convenience. Neither should stop you.

Process is a crucial lever of power. You shouldn't accept the one you inherited any more than you would only run plays from the last coach's playbook. A careful re-think of your team's approach, applied with a light touch, can have a massively scaled impact.

Default Roles

For most of the game's history, an offense in American Football relied on a good Fullback. Fullbacks blocked the middle linebacker, clearing the way for Running Backs and they took their own handoffs to keep the defense honest. They were a staple of run first and option offenses built around the I formation and its derivatives. Without a good Fullback, an offense couldn't run the ball, score or win. Until 1958, Fullbacks were often the highest scoring players in the NFL.

And then the game changed. In the 1980s, teams began passing more, and started fielding fast, pass-catching Receivers in place of their lumbering Fullbacks. Defenses responded by changing their own personnel to counter the aerial threat. An offensive revolution in football followed. Today, Fullbacks are a novelty in the NFL and many teams don't even have one on the roster.

The essence of Football didn't change. Players still ran, threw, caught and blocked to score points. The rules stayed pretty much the same. Innovation occurred because coaches, limited by the number of players they could have on the field, re-imagined how to run, throw, catch and block to get more versatility and productivity out of the eleven players. And as a result, they quit playing Fullbacks.

The decline of Fullbacks in football happened because the game constrains teams to eleven players at a time. If a coach wanted more wide receivers on the field, someone else had to sit on the bench. The rules of the game prevent role proliferation.

Creative teams do not work under such clear constraints. Unlike football, zombie roles develop over time as work changes, and the considered decisions that lead to certain positions go unexamined. Financial success lets your team get fat. Levels, disciplines and specializations accumulate.

This accumulation is a form of entropy. It drains your budget for talent, constraining your ability to hire and promote. The roles that aren't optimized for your vision are occupying a seat better used by someone else. Their well meaning contribution distracts from the work you want to be doing, and the way you want to be doing it. They take up your time and attention.

As a creative leader, you should always be evaluating the makeup of your team. What skills are you missing that would improve it? What ones sit unused? What work could be consolidated into a more robust role? What roles are the Fullbacks you don't need to run your offense?

Your vision will demand its own strange combinations of skills. You will need a team that fits to succeed. Don't let an unchallenged default role be the thing that stops you.

PLAYBOOK

I t doesn't say great things about my own creativity that the thing I will be most remembered for from my eight years at Digitas is a format. Part strategy, part creative vision, part planning document, the thing we called the "North Star" became as much a part of the design culture as sharpies and post it notes. Account reps sold them faster than we could staff them. PMs asserted, "We could NorthStar that" in planning meetings. The outputs were consistent across offices and teams, tracking to the same general timeline, quality and cost. Repeat clients asked for them by name like a flavor of GirlScout cookies. Both approach and output, the NorthStar was the Design team's bread and butter play.

A couple years after adopting the North Star as our preferred method, I felt affirmed when Jake Knapp and Google Ventures published "Sprint", their guide to running design sprints. Sprint's contribution was taking the labored and often open ended aspects of user centered design processes and suggesting ways to structure and time box them. It's a Playbook about a set of very effective plays, in service of a specific kind of design problem. Google Ventures went on to run a cottage industry helping organizations run it.

I'm including these anecdotes because in many creative organizations there is resistance to anything smelling of process that borders on primal fear. A skin crawling sense that "process" leads to putting well-calibrated chaos teams in some kind of paint by numbers factory. A belief that structure is the road to mediocrity because creativity doesn't work like that.

Some of this fear is well placed. You can't say that on Monday we're going to get inspired and at 2PM on Friday we're going to have the idea together. No amount of over-managed meetings, check-ins or forced reviews can wring a creative thought out of a stuck team. But, some of the revulsion is diva behavior from a capability who often wants to be left alone to "do their thing" without accountability for when they don't. In your role, you do need a schedule for the work, but it's impossible to schedule the individual breakthroughs within it.

My solution to this has been to think less in terms of rigid processes and more in terms of a flexible playbook. Process implies a stepwise linearity. Something repeatable from beginning to end across all kinds of problems. If you work in a creative driven field, you will already know that rigid processes don't work. What does work is having the broad outline of a schedule and your own set of plays to get from the beginning to the end. Plays like, how do you structure ideation? Where do you collect unorganized research? When do you synthesize it and into what? What is enough work to express the shape of an idea? How do you put a look or a voice through its paces? How do you decide what idea to pursue and what to cut?

If you find yourself reinventing the answers to these questions all the time, you are making your life a lot harder than it needs to be.

You need a playbook because what your team does is uneven and nonlinear. Sometimes you will spiral between discovery, ideation and exploration for weeks without landing a solution. Other times someone will show up on day one with an outstanding concept that needs support and validation. Process doesn't know what to do with that. Leading creativity requires having the tools to recognize each situation and activating your team in the right way to move through it.

Your playbook will make the repeatable parts of creativity boring in the best possible way. At minimum, having a set of acceptable outputs for project milestones is clarifying. Telling your team to build a customer journey, make a mood board or ideate a few concepts and know what to expect and when, is an underrated thing. Saying, "Make one of these" takes the guesswork out of an inherently intangible business, working both as a jumping off point and as a quality baseline.

A playbook structure truly doesn't take much. Just a few shared methods and form factors make a world of difference when aligning expectations. It takes the debate out of method and form factors and frees teams up to focus on solving the problems in the work. And it gives you the flexibility you need to lead in all kinds of variable situations throughout the excitement and the chaos of creative problem solving.

LEADERSHIP AND LEADS

"Success is rarely the work of a single leader; leaders work best in partnership with other leaders."

- STANLEY MCCHRYSTAL

One of the funniest misconceptions junior creatives carry is that teammates will ever be impressed by their job title. That somehow adding "Director" to their email signature equates to others being inspired by their ideas or listening more closely to their feedback. On a team shaped by competition for ideas and craft skills, titles only raise the bar to clear for respect. He's a Creative Director now? Shoulder shrug and eyebrow raise. K.

As you build your team and scale your influence, you will need to recruit and cultivate leaders and it can be easy to start thinking of them in terms of roles. An Associate Creative Director here, a Group creative director there. Financial and corporate structures reinforce this. Reporting structures and funded roles act as the building blocks for org design. And then suddenly you're making the same mistake as your junior team who thinks the big title will confer respect - because in truth, leadership and job titles have nothing to do with each other.

Leadership is ownership and accountability and doing the hard or right things without being asked. Helping struggling teammates, fighting for quality and pushing to make everything better. It's being someone others are drawn to when they are vulnerable or unsure. It's being the one who brings the weather.

You can't title yourself or anyone else into it.

Like creativity, leadership is a muscle built from repeated use, exposure and feedback. You should encourage it in every role and at every level. On your team this is very much a *you* problem. Only you can decide how you will loosen your grip. Cultivate leaders by giving up control yourself. Tell teammates they own something, and be ok with that. Insist on quality while accepting that no one will give the same direction or make the same decisions as you. Every time you reverse a decision they make, you subtly undermine their ability to lead in the future. Every time you let a bad decision go, you undermine work quality.

Getting this right is going to be hard.

But when you do get it right, the dynamic changes. Teams with strong leadership qualities work on their front foot. They act with conviction and purpose. They're happier. They push harder. And over time, teammates emerge who others look to. Who others ask for. Who bring the calm or the energy - who bring the weather as the situation demands. Whose leadership muscles are stronger than the rest.

And then you know where to put the Director titles.

JOB DESCRIPTIONS

Among the various ways people try to pin down the intangible bits that make a great creative team member, the detailed job description (JD) must be the most irritating. You are recruiting and growing multifaceted people whose job is to redefine, transform, and create moments of beauty, awe, delight and interest. There is not a checklist for getting there.

I don't know of many creative leaders asking for JDs. The detailed job description is a blunt filter used by your recruiters and their algorithms to weed applicants out. Online job postings attract large numbers of inbound requests, even at middling companies. At large successful companies, like Google or Apple, applications are in the millions. The volume drives demand for ever more detailed descriptions and criteria to help shrink the candidate pools and a proliferation of JDs that read like house party playlists is the result.

If you work in a large company, well intentioned recruiters will try to take this off your plate so you should fire up a browser and have a look at your company's job postings. Software and media requirements age like fish in the sun. Listing every media platform and tool in the Adobe suite is not a useful talent screen. Recruiters' inexpert choices can skew your candidate pool in some tragic-comic ways. After puzzling over why every candidate for a role insisted on emphasizing their InDesign experience (a tool that was not part of our stack) I discovered it was a point of emphasis, along with other tools we never used, in our published JD. A copy and paste error, keeping print know how alive at a digital agency into perpetuity. During another candidate search, we shrugged for months at why we weren't seeing any applications before realizing the description read as a convincing career obituary.

When recruiting creatives, filtering out bad fits is less important than attracting the good ones and the good ones aren't going to show up as a checklist. The good ones are shifty characters and hard to pigeon hole or replicate. The good ones want to be inspired. Your problem isn't applicant volume, it's candidate quality. With apologies to the recruiting team, write a Shackleton description and let the recruiters filter by hand.

If detailed job descriptions act as a way of getting bad talent in the door, detailed role descriptions help keep it there. Among Creative team members, an insistence on a detailed role description is a red flag. If this were low skill, low pay labor it would be reasonable to want to know the full set of chores required at the position. After you serve the last customer, you clean the fryer, count out the register, prep for the next day and you get to go home.

That is not and never will be a role on a creative team. Variety, fluidity, dynamism, a commitment to lifelong learning, tinkering and discovery are the essence of the job. The list of things to do is ever changing and never ending. There is no comprehensive description.

A team member who is asking for details of their role is either trying to limit their scope or check boxes to make a case for promotion. The latter comes from a misunderstanding of promotion criteria (see related chapter). The former from laziness.

Contrary to what you would expect, the details create inefficiency and confusion about who does or is responsible for what. They invite people to opt out of things that aren't in their narrow niche. They achieve complexity without adding value. They lead to balkanization and defensiveness. They are a trap. The more you say, the more you are expected to. If you are detailed and omit something, others can, and will, assume the omission is intentional. That it's not their job. Don't fall into the trap. Make job and role descriptions a sweeping call to arms and work out the details by working with the talented people who answer.

It is worth pausing here to note that mine is a minority view. If you ask any HR professional or read any management best practice literature, you will find that one of the most important factors in employee satisfaction is knowing what is expected of them. Itemized role descriptions are a popular way of accomplishing this. But I can't square this with the tolerance for ambiguity creativity requires.

LINKED CAPABILITIES

While I hope this book reads as a reminder to control everything you can, this chapter is a pause to acknowledge that a lot of your success will depend on things you can't control. At least not directly. Your organization's broader design will impact culture, posture and work product in ways that are hard to foresee. The decisions about how and when different capabilities interface, what makes up a team and who leads it, are at the heart of org design. Unless you are in the C-suite (why are you reading this?) these are things you will inherit and have to work within.

So now you're in a bigger boat, with a lot of people who do things you don't, who report to someone else and have their own measures of success and quality. As you think about your team in this larger system, you must confront the reality that all these other people can create a ceiling for your potential. This ceiling is a lot lower than you might think, and it's tied to the nature of creativity in business as weak-link work.

A system of people is considered either strong-link or weak-link depending on what leads to its success. Strong-link systems are as strong as the strongest individual on the team. Weak-link ones are as strong as the weakest. Malcom Gladwell illustrates the difference in an episode of his podcast, Revisionist History, by comparing soccer to basketball. "You will never see one person dribble the soccer ball from one end of the field to the other but...LeBron James does not need anyone else to touch the ball to win." Soccer is a weak-link system. Basketball is a strong-link one.

Creativity in business is a weak-link system and the weakest link in your creative enterprise might not be on the creative team. If you work in app design and the worst team member is the lead developer, you are cruising to a one star rating. If you are producing social video content and your producer is mediocre, so is your output. If you are leading digital transformation and your strategist is a hack, so is everything that follows. A Bauhaus quality creative department can be undone by one lackluster teammate in a linked capability.

Creative work is enabled and supported by a raft of other capabilities in a larger team structure, and if you want to have anything more than a pretty pitch deck you are going to need them to be as good as the team you build yourself. You can't take over their teams, so you might be tempted to take over parts of their roles. I have written more than my share of strategies. Staffed too many hacky designers masquerading as developers. These are dead ends that will frustrate everyone and expose you trying to do things you don't understand. Avoid them. Instead, focus on the following principle when evaluating their work.

Visibility is not the same as importance.

This seems obvious until you think about where time gets spent surrounding projects. The creative work receives the lion's share of praise and criticism in any assignment. Creative will get more flack, more applause, more scrutiny and more aggressive management from others for the simple reason that everyone can see it.

I have still never been to a company town hall where someone presented a really elegant line of code or adaptable project plan. I have never seen the strategy deck appear as the marquee in a press release or Fast Company article. I have been to very few awards shows where tech was invited to the banquet table.

We all know our work is the sum of a lot of contributors but our lizard brains forget it as soon as things go right or wrong. Your job is to remind everyone how this really works. To revisit the invisible work of all the linked capabilities at major project milestones, not only at the end when you're assigning blame or champagne. Make sure that even if you can't control them, you scrutinize all the other links in the chain the same way you would the final edit or typeface choice.

Creativity is a weak-link job. Remember to shine a bright light on every link in the chain.

FOUR GOOD
MEETINGS

Like all moral people of good character, I am skeptical of meetings. Past a handful of teammates and half an hour or so, they make my skin ache. Whenever possible, I mind shift to somewhere or something else, trying to think out the details of actual work I'll be coming back to when the meeting finally ends. If I'm forced to pay attention, I tend to hijack them, running through the scheduled programming, jamming any relevant topic I can think of into them, and then canceling as many future meetings as I can. What's the 3 PM? Can we do it now? How about the 4?. One good meeting can kill days of the things.

In this, I am not alone. A boss of mine once led the team in creating the Cost of Meeting App (COMA) that averaged the hourly rates of participants before showing the real time cost of the meeting as a ticking dollar amount over animated flames. Until the joke got old, someone in the peanut gallery of an over scheduled get together would reliably break it out, and let it spin and burn on the conference room table while project managers laughed uncomfortably.

The meetings did not get smaller or less frequent.

Meeting hate is up there with open office hate and timesheet hate in the pantheon of detested work trappings. Among the makers, saying you are pro-meeting puts you so far outside the mainstream you might as well be a narc. So it's with some regret that I write the following: you are going to need some meetings for career and team management and they are going to have to recur on a set schedule.

Having these meetings will often feel like nothing - and that makes them feel like wasted time. It isn't. The way I learned their value was by not having them, when what I gained in time back I more than lost in teammates alienated by stilted annual career conversations, teammates who's relationship with me only existed in the flow of project work, teammates who had no venue for raising concerns and entire teams without visibility into what was happening with one another and why.

A cadence of the following four seems to do the trick.

Your Boss

This one's for you, and you need to drive it. Actively managing your boss, staying on their page about priorities and getting ahead of them on problems is critical. Don't wait for them to schedule this. Pick a time, get organized with an agenda and stick to your cadence.

Your Direct Reports (check-ins)

Check-ins build and maintain relationships and give you a venue for feedback and career conversations outside the formal annual review process. Management books can give you every kind of script and agenda for how to structure these, but my experience is that they are best when they are fluid and informal. If you're doing them right you often won't be talking about work at all.

I have always found frequency to be a major check-in limitation. In her lauded management book Radical Candor, author Kim Scott recommends checking in with each of your direct reports for an hour every week. Maybe that works outside the confines of the billable hour, but for those of us with a timesheet to do, half an hour every two weeks keeps things close but not repetitive. Whatever your schedule is, do your best to keep it.

Your Leads

A reliably useful way to spend a half hour is a meeting with anyone on your team who is leading a work stream. What is the status for each project? Are there any blockers? How's the team doing? Is there any work we should all see? Is there anything any of us can do to help? Bringing your leadership class together is a good step towards building scale and reinforcing their roles. It also lets them benefit from the support and the scrutiny of their peer group.

Your Entire Team

All-team meetings are hard to generalize. They're good for announcements that provoke questions, and for truing up on values, initiatives and other work everyone should be aware of. The bigger your team, the bigger the commitment required and the bigger the time wastage. What you do for a team of twenty doesn't scale to a team of two hundred. Whatever your size, they are best when they are as short, infrequent and as scheduled as you can make them. You will know you are doing them right when you are running out of time and people leave wanting more.

SEATING

"A new scientific truth does not triumph by convincing its opponents and making them see the light, but rather because its opponents eventually die."

- MAX PLANCK

I began my creative career as a junior freelancer at Digitas New York. At the time the agency was independent, headquartered in Boston, and growing fast with a few hundred employees scattered across five floors of a century old building on Park Avenue. The late stage cube farm seating was a far cry from the open-plan offices of today. Junior creatives occupied the center of the floorplan in a jumble of semi-transparent, not quite cubicles called "pods". Surrounding us, the outer walls held the offices of mid-tier managers, (single, shared or corner assigned based on title) along with access to all the windows. The inconsistency of the pods felt like peeking through a tree canopy - always watched but never able to see anything. Grouped in threes in a faux organic pattern, finding someone's desk even using the laminated wall maps felt like a quest. The noise of competing phone conversations and an enormous printer running non-stop was only broken by employee searchers shouting for someone to stand up so they could locate their seat.

Sometime during my second year, leadership announced we would move to client-based seating. Before this, teams organized by discipline (Account, PM, Engineering, etc.). This being my first real job, I never thought about seating beyond the number of times I had to shuttle up and down the fire stairs (the elevators were rush hour slow) for work reviews. I heard the news and wasn't sure I cared. Others *were* sure. The news was met with relief by the Account teams who were freed to integrate capabilities around their lanes of business and act as the mini-CEOs they always wanted to be, and with apocalyptic pronouncements from the creative leadership about massive quality declines and the death of creative culture. "This place is over", a reliably popular sentiment from a certain kind of mid-level creative in any era, became the catch phrase conversational sign off of the department.

The new arrangement stuck, and the efficiency and quality of the various accounts improved while the culture tacked more towards management consultancy than agency. It was my introduction to the seating wars, a bizarre and heartfelt conflict that continues to this day. It is not hyperbole to say that of all the things I have seen get people emotional in a work environment, none has been as charged as where people sit. Bonuses, layoffs, client resignations, pandemic pay cuts and company acquisitions have all been moments experienced one way or another in my corporate career. Many more than once. None has matched the red hot passion of seating. If there is a third rail of American corporate life, it is where people park themselves during the work day.

A few years after the seat-pocalypse at Digitas, I moved on to a small (one hundred person or so) shop attempting a turnaround. Accounts were in decline and creative quality was uneven. A new Executive Creative Director joined to right the ship. He wasn't there a week before he moved the company from client to team-based seating. The Account leadership howled. How could they be expected to deliver work if they couldn't oversee the team?

Why would we put up such an arbitrary barrier to efficiency? How would they maintain control? Shortly after the move, a reinvigorated creative department went on a tear, winning both new business and awards at a clip that wouldn't have been imaginable a few months before.

Twenty years into my career in agency land, I'm ready to call the tradeoff. Neither arrangement is perfect. The choice is between efficiency and creativity. Cross functional teams organized around a client or work area (feature teams) gain and keep deep, problem specific expertise that lets them move through work with few preventable mistakes. In agencies, they understand the nuances of a specific client and avoid the traps that come with stepping on organizational land mines. This approach prizes certainty and lack of drama. It's why in-house creative teams are usually organized this way.

By contrast, seating by capability (a studio model) maximizes interactions within a capability at the expense of interactions with others. This might sound like a recipe for an echo chamber but there is an upside. Creatives who sit with other creatives become a hive of technique and idea sharing. Designers ask "Will you look at this? Something isn't working." while tilting a screen towards critical eyes. Writers try lines for a laugh before re-working. You could argue that this would and should still happen with mixed capability seating, but you would be wrong. Craft skill improves when it's pushed by craft skill and if you want to have an opinion at the moment of creation, being a maker is the price of entry. No one is looking for enlightened craft feedback from the Finance team.

Whether to sit by capability or account was the first front of the seating wars. The efficiency vs creativity front. If you worked through the aughts and post-aughts you can guess the second. During the 1990s a revolution in office design swept through work culture. Lead by the tech platforms, workers moved from the relentless cubicle wastelands with managers sequestered in their power-status offices into the egalitarian world of the open plan. Seats became "free address" letting employees sit where they wanted. The personal shrines we built at our desks were torn down and put into lockers. Flexibility arrived to create a new age of collaboration and redefine the modern work environment.

The shitstorm that followed became a generational marker. Open offices with flexible seating were blamed for everything from the spread of disease to the death of attention spans and personal productivity. They were accused of reducing the individual into interchangeable corporate cogs. People complained about predictable things like the noise (I assure you, the cubes, pods and others were also loud). And people complained about unexpected things like not having a place for family photos. In any given month from about 2010 to 2020 at least one business section or professional magazine included a breathless article about how these work spaces were killing us all. If you happened to lead a team, someone always forwarded it your way.

Reactions on my own team covered the full spectrum. I had dynamic managers who I expected to embrace open plan working reduced to glassy eyed fits about losing their office. I saw introverts who I thought might walk out in protest lit up from the easy human contact. Engaged employees strapped on noise canceling headphones and vanished in plain sight. Professional complaint forums like GlassDoor and LinkedIn never tired of the topic.

When I started writing this, the open vs closed front in the seating war seemed to have been decided. Many - maybe most - employees found them loud and distracting but open plans would be the office configuration for the foreseeable future. Whatever else they were, they were cheaper, cramming in more employees per square foot than other configurations. Money has a way of winning arguments, and the money was on open-plan no matter what the yells of protest were.

And then along came COVID.

Driven by the pandemic office exodus and all it wrought, the latest front in the seating wars is between those fighting for a return to office and those who want to continue working from home. The breathless articles are flying through the business trades again. The vitriolic LinkedIn comments are unreadable. While I couldn't have imagined doing our version of creative work remotely in 2020, to say it's routine in 2023 undersells it - it's both better and more efficient. So while I have my own thoughts about how this will all turn out for work culture (money wins arguments and commercial leases are just CAPEX waiting to be re-allocated) after three editions of the seating war sucking up my career energy I've reached a thought on peace.

Seat by chaos.

It only matters at the margins where people sit. You will never recoup the time and goodwill you lose fighting about it in productivity or quality gains. In the connected era, the difference between a teammate on Mars and a teammate at your desk is almost no difference at all. Embrace the flexibility gained by letting go. Hug the chaos with both hands. There are fights to fight for creativity. The seating wars isn't one.

PROMOTION CRITERIA

Raises and promotions are finite resources. Every raise or promotion for one team member comes at the expense of another. Along with hiring and casting they are the most important people decisions you will make on your team.

Without a clear definition of what merits a promotion, managers tend to fall back on promoting based on a combination of perceived fairness and fear of attrition. This is reactive. Team members will argue otherwise but there's nothing fair about promoting someone because a peer got a promotion or because they have been in a role for a long period of time. There's also nothing wrong with a certain amount of attrition, as long as the people leaving are people you weren't going to promote based on merit.

I use the following prompts to clarify the promotion conversation. They are the same for every person in every role below those who manage offices. I share them with every new hire and force every raise or promotion discussion through them. While not perfect, having a consistent set of criteria to fall back on has been a huge help managing expectations within my teams. When someone meets this standard, it makes it very clear when I should be advocating for them to move up.

What to care about

1. What work did they do that is amazing or unique?
2. What kudos did they get from stakeholder or leadership?
3. Are they the best at their level in their role?
4. Do they do more than asked?
5. Do they make the team they work with better?
6. Are they doing the job at the next level?
7. Does their promotion make sense for the organization of our team?
8. Do others look to them for leadership?

What not to care about

1. Time in role
2. How much they think they deserve it

TOOLS

"Technology changes faster than people do."

-      DEREK THOMPSON, HIT MAKERS

Y ou can't be too paranoid or obsessive about the software your team uses. Of all the defaults, tools are the one companies seem most inclined to dissuade a creative leader from thinking about. That's what we have IT for. We bought two hundred seats. We're good. Do your thing.

Do not accept this premise.

The best tools are force multipliers. The difference between the latest and those a year or two old is hours of collective wasted time. Modern software devours repetitive tasks and enables scaled quality and collaboration. It creates marginal gains that add up to significant ones across a team and over time. It acts as a signal of your own modernity to potential recruits. Your tool stack is a very big deal and it cannot be left to someone in procurement.

When people first started talking about the 'Consumerization of IT' they were talking about hardware. We wanted our iPhones goddamnit, who was IT to tell us we couldn't have them? Now we're neck deep in the mass fragmentation of our workflow. We're hot swapping software almost daily in a creative tools arms race.

As I write this, the Adobe CC icons are gathering dust in my dock. I still have MSOffice for some reason, but I spend a minute cursing and force-quitting anytime I accidentally open any of it. For documents and spreadsheets we only use Google docs. IT would not approve these tools if I bothered to ask. I haven't, and I encourage you not to either. If your boss or your IT department are going to slow modern tool adoption, you will have to work around them.

We have entered the era of the disposable tech stack. Long gone are the days when an agency procurement department could just negotiate a few hundred seats of the Adobe suite and let-er-rip. The new stack is made of cheap, niche, power tools that are more powerful and more interoperable than what came before. The new stack is networked and acts as a collaborative backbone. The new stack is cloud, subscription and releasing improvements almost daily.

The tools that stick have low switching costs and no maintenance. The best ones (At the time of this writing - Figma stands out) have robust ecosystems of developers building extensions that let them act like productivity platforms. Re-training happens on Youtube and TikTok.

To embrace this reality, the challenge will be to accept the death of command and control software planning, and to find ways to support a vibrant and organic software ecosystem. You will have to absorb constant, rapid change in the software stacks on the team. It's going to be messy. It's going to feel haphazard. With the business of creativity so defined by software, that's going to have to be ok.

A GOOD RIVAL

"What are you doing to beat Ohio State today?"

- SIGN HANGING IN THE WEIGHT ROOM OF THE UNIVERSITY
OF MICHIGAN FOOTBALL TEAM

"Father Divine said to always establish a 'we/they': an 'us,' and an enemy on the outside," explained Laura Johnston Kohl, our Jonestown vet. The goal is to make your people feel like they have all the answers, while the rest of the world is not just foolish, but inferior."

- AMANDA MONTELL, CULTISH: THE LANGUAGE OF
FANATICISM

This is a hack, but it works. You will have read about the importance of being mission driven. Of having a direction of travel for your team and communicating it. You know you are on a path to change the world together. To put a dent in your corner of the universe. And if you make what you are all trying to do clear enough, often enough, everyone will get on your page and you will get there together.

This is probably the right way to do it, but it isn't the fastest or only one. Even good missions can sound a little soft. New directions lack urgency. You end up using words like 'best', 'first' and 'only', and they feel just as empty as they are. Getting a team to internalize a nebulous future vision takes careful authorship on your part and a lot of repetition. It takes a thoughtful step out of corporate jargon into a believable and aspirational place. More than that, it takes time, and in this job, you don't have much.

The hack is to pick a fight.

Stop being high minded. Look around for something to be against and declare it the enemy. Announce it. Remind people of it. The more successful and well known it is, the better. Now you have something to anchor to. Something to color in the gaps in your vision. Who are we? We're the anti-them.

A good rival isn't an abstraction, it's a competitor of some kind - and business is full of competition. Tangible competition creates a little bit of fear and anxiety. Are they better than us? Are we going to lose to them? With the right people on your team, those questions will nag. They will foment their own lite anxiety. They will be the reason to try another version or learn a new skill. They will be over every collective shoulder, every time people think about easing up.

A good rival helps focus your purpose. Early in my career I inherited an agency design team that while good, lacked a strong identity. They had recently lost a pitch to another agency who at the time was getting a lot of attention in New York. They were in the trade publications and at the award shows and working on the cooler brands. They were recruiting our best people and announcing expansions into new markets. If you couldn't get a job there, they were under your bed and in your closet.

I wanted my team to be something modern and untraditional. At the time a lot of process and creative dogma got in the way of what should have been shorter, sharper engagements and solutions. I was asking the team to change the tools and techniques they used, to upskill in some areas, and to stop spending time in others. I was asking a lot, and it was only partially taking.

And then I started asking for it through the lens of our competition. When asking for the team to be less formal, dogmatic and methodical I name dropped them. When pushing us to take bigger creative risks and make more emotional arguments - I made sure to say that they would never. They had a mythology in our space at that moment, and it lined up flush with what I didn't want us to be. I built up the straw man. They were going to do it this way, so we would beat them doing it that way. They were the other by which we defined ourselves.

Us vs them is the stuff of cults, outgroups and challenger brands. It is an old tribal dynamic and it recurs because it works. I'm still surprised how well it did. We leaned hard into our own strengths, winning business and awards. We became our own thing, with our own identity and culture. Our competition probably never knew it, but they had been the perfect rival for us.

Being against something isn't ever as powerful as being for it but, if you need a shortcut, the sharp relief and competitive dread of a common enemy is a good one.

IT'S ABOUT TIME

O f all the petty power dynamics that play out in a creative team, the tendency for bad managers to use time as an instrument of control is probably the most destructive. Your time is not more important than the people you work with. When you signal you believe otherwise, you are advertising your own insecurity and inviting any self respecting person with the misfortune of reporting to you to find another job.

Schedule bullying is everywhere in creative professions. An intra-generational hazing ritual that refuses to die out. A Creative Director I worked with was notorious for spending a day with clients before arriving back at the office at six in the evening to start reviewing work. She would force the entire team to stay until she was satisfied, whether or not the work was theirs. At one shop so much dinner was ordered and expensed that the finance department flagged it as potential fraud. Too often, it's not seen as any big deal. Seven o'clock regroups or Sunday morning calls are added without warning or apology.

When I was just starting out, I assumed leadership had good intentions. I felt lucky to have a job, and I would do what it took to keep it. With more experience I saw our busyness was more often bad planning, self-importance or both. A lot of the time I spent in those days was waiting around. Waiting for feedback, for a review, for someone senior to approve whatever we'd made. Sometimes we were told to wait until late at night with nothing to do, on the outside chance some reviewer would want something added or changed. A lot of that waiting was for nothing. When someone cracked and called it a night, someone else would mumble "half day?" at their back on the way out. Even bad cultures become self-enforcing.

There is only so much of this people will take, and the more talented they are, the less of it. At some point during a late night waiting at the creative DMV, your team will figure out you have no respect for their time. Why go to all the trouble of recruiting and organizing incredible people just to demotivate them like this? The second you are happy with the work, send your team home. The second you don't need anything else from someone, tell that team member thanks and good night. If you are staying late once in a while for good reasons, they will shrug and get on with it. Crunch time happens. But, face time is toxic. Their time is their life. A good leader won't waste it.

TEAM

TALENT STRATEGY

T he 1980s were a good time to be a Real Madrid soccer fan. In a dominant run, Madrid won five consecutive La Liga titles and two UEFA cups playing their unique, precision rapid-passing version of the beautiful game. Madrid's success owed a lot to their commitment to a particular brand of soccer, and their approach to the talent needed to make it work. Madrid was not built by shopping the player market for the best international stars and bringing them together as a super team. It wasn't finding undervalued or overlooked players in other clubs and giving them playing time. Instead, it was growing its own stars using a committed youth league called La Fabrica (the Factory). Talented players were identified at a young age and shaped in the details of Madrid's system. They weren't grown to be soccer players - they were grown to be Madrid soccer players. Madrid did not compete for talent on the open market, because La Fabrica created it.

This was not a happy accident. La Fabrica is an example of a talent strategy; A plan for attracting, developing and deploying a specific kind of talent for a competitive advantage.

The example of La Fabrica is instructive because of how total and committed it is as a way of addressing constraint and opportunity. Faced with the constraint of prohibitive star salaries and the opportunity to run a disruptive passing offense, every facet of the club was designed to minimize the former and maximize the latter. Recruiting focused on affordable junior talent allowing for the greatest development time in the Madrid system at the least cost. Having more junior recruits created a volume of players to choose from (a hedge against bad scouting, injury and the like) to fill rare roles on the top team.

The La Fabrica strategy systematizes recruiting, firing, development and promotion as a set of linked decisions. The view of talent is multifaceted. The systems surrounding it are deliberate. The result is an organization with an abundance of human capital ready to execute its approach. Clear-eyed organizations familiar with the constraints and opportunities of their talent market have developed an endless variety of approaches worth learning from.

Before being acquired by Amazon, Zappos competed on their unique customer service culture. To preserve it, they focused recruiting on malleable junior talent, with Founder Tony Hsieh stating, "Ideally we would never recruit anyone above entry level." Hsieh's Flywheel approach was creating an environment where leadership, values and culture were so strong that inexperience became an asset - one that allowed new hires to more quickly adopt the Zappos way. This approach had the added advantage of clearing the career path for other employees. When your recruiting is focused on mid or senior levels, every hire enters the team in competition with the others at the same level. Paths for promotion that open through attrition close off, alienating team members farther down the hierarchy. Promoting from within reinforces culture and boosts retention.

For a counterpoint Strategy, consider the All-Star approach. Flush with investment dollars while on a hockey stick growth path into the Entertainment industry, Netflix's executive team famously asked "What if everyone on our team was an A-Player?" This question is at the heart of the Silicon Valley - famous deck, the Netflix Culture Manifesto. In it, then Chief Talent Officer Patty McCord describes the standards of excellence sought within the company - no "B players" - and their talent approach for removing under-performing employees as a way of reaching it. This may sound too obvious to even be considered a strategy - who doesn't want to work with "A players"? - but Netflix's total commitment to the approach stood out. Few companies are comfortable operating with a stated policy of "adequate performance gets a generous severance package". Fewer still are willing to spend whatever is necessary to take money off the table when recruiting. The willingness to do what others simply won't, even if it's obvious, is a competitive advantage.

Following the wars in Iraq and Afghanistan, the US Marine Corps began changing their force posture to better match future deployments. Planners imagined future conflicts where groups of Marines on extended missions might have to operate scattered over huge areas in relative isolation - islands in the Pacific for example - relying more on high tech equipment than brute force or numbers. The unskilled teenager that forms the traditional bedrock of Marine recruiting doesn't fit this mission. Starting in late 2021, the Marines announced their new approach to talent - Talent Management 2030 - which would recruit a smaller number of Marines with higher selection criteria, before training them to be more independent minded. Putting greater value on "Military judgment", Marine recruiters expanded reenlistment incentives and started recruiting mid-career professionals. They strategically changed their approach to recruitment and development.

Each of these examples is total. Mission, recruitment, training, and advancement are linked by design.

Contrast this with the typical creative recruitment team. The default approach to talent is a kind of local control. An opening appears and a hiring manager is empowered to influence the job description, vet candidates, organize interviews and make the decision on whether or not to offer a candidate. As this plays out at scale, a team or entire company is a cumulation of individual hires directed by individual managers. Companies add checks for quality and fit by adding layers of decision making on the hire, with rounds of successive interviews or approvals. Sometimes a creative executive will act as a final arbiter on the decision to move forward.

This entire approach is reactive. Waiting for a need to materialize before vetting candidates. Waiting for a candidate pool to discuss quality. To the extent that a master plan exists, it is a level setting of selection criteria given to recruiters. While it may keep talent decisions close to where a team member will work, it misses the chance to line up talent acquisition, development and product strategy.

Individual hiring decisions are important, but examining talent in its totality can lead to real competitive advantage. Take the time to write a strategy for talent on your creative team, and use it to drive the tactical decisions that follow. This is your factory. Design it well.

HIRING FOR A VUCA WORLD

"Hire the kinds of people clients don't have and wouldn't dream of having."

- DAVID OGILVY

The three hiring criteria I encounter most often are skillset, experience and cultural fit. So ingrained they don't merit discussion, managers and recruiters filter for teammates they want to be around, who solve an immediate need, and have solved it before somewhere else. Nothing too complicated here. If you need someone to design apps, you could do worse than hiring someone who has designed apps before. If you can spend ten hours at a time with them and not want to scream into a pillow? Bonus. These team members get up to speed fast and fill an obvious need. And then they become obsolete.

The problem with this most common recruiting criteria has to do with the changing nature of creative work. Form factors and the tools we use to create for them are turning over at a blistering speed. In my own world we went from designing web sites to apps to voice to messaging, wearables and augmented reality, all in a span of about five years. No new medium completely displaced the old, they just stacked up. Each with their own context of use, customer preferences, design and production quirks. And with them came new tools. Unique authoring environments for Augmented Reality. A design tool arms race for the web. A growing mandate for rapid change in exponents, not increments.

Today, you can tell any creative person you hire with candor that the job they do on day one will not be the same for more than two years at a time, ever, for the entirety of their career. The media, the devices, the creative tools, the team and the processes will all change, often at the same time.

This is what the literature calls a Volatile Uncertain Complex and Ambiguous (VUCA) environment. It's a world defined by variability and constant change. Needs materialize in months or weeks instead of decades. Entire skill sets blink in and out of relevance almost overnight. To human beings who prefer routine and comfort, this change is deeply unsettling.

There isn't a magic band aid that that will protect your creative team from the waves of technological and cultural change we are all swimming through. But if you can't stop it or anticipate it, you can still build it into your recruiting strategy. Before you were filling a role trying to solve a specific problem. Now, not knowing what's ahead, you're looking for versatility and adaptability. Experience with a current tool or technique is less important than a spoken curiosity, and ability to try new ones. First principles and theory form a foundation for an infinite and ever changing set of craft skills.

Put this into practice by changing your recruiting approach and interview questions. Look for candidates from classic programs with deep foundations instead of those from portfolio schools. Scour applicants for the career switchers and the side hustlers.

Ask candidates what they are reading and listening to. What the last new thing they learned was and whether they took a class or taught themselves. Ask them how long it took them to apply it and whether they ever got good. Ask them how they solve problems. Don't bother asking about the specifics of a role you have today. You won't need them for it for very long anyway.

A LEARNING CULTURE

What will you make in the future? In three years ? in five? What tool will change the way you create next year ? What new medium will your audience be spending their time on? What will happen in culture? In design? What will be meaningfully different?

Driven by technology, the pace of change in any industry today is exponential. Whereas an editor may have worked in broadcast for 30 years from the 1950s through the 1980s and experienced only small updates to technology and techniques, beginning in the 1990's, the Internet unleashed a massive fragmentation in mediums, formats, tools, trends and subcultures. Instead of the next big thing, there were just more things. This revolution is not slowing. Instead of small advancements and periodic skill updates, your team will face an endless onslaught of accelerating radical change.

Though we often see ourselves as a different class, creatives are just like anyone else - we fear change. And so we resist it. During my own career I have seen several waves of Ad creatives trying to manifest a return to the Mad Men days of broadcast TV while their friends in Media Planning patted them on the head and bought more digital inventory. Have watched the UX wave rise, crest and fade while a small group of evangelists refused to see that their career had become an ingredient skill in a designer's toolkit and not the stand-alone profession they imagined. I have watched writers spin on a sentence of performance copy when a free generator could write it better, faster and in multiples.

Each in their own way retreated into a defensive crouch around the purity of their craft, hoping they could extract it from its modern application. They hid behind concept and theory and derided application as production. If they didn't want to learn it, they called it a fad. Or they made fun of it. The changes happened anyway.

In this volatile future one truth exists: the team that learns the fastest, wins. You will not be able to hire for the hard skills required tomorrow. Taste and judgment are evergreen but insufficient without craft skill. You will not have a team with timeless trades applied through the life of their careers. And you will not be able to put a training bandaid on the open wound of change. Instead, every member of your team, and the whole of the team itself, will have to renew and apply their skills or face irrelevance.

Your job is to encourage them. To cultivate experimentation and knowledge sharing. To stoke a healthy disregard for the old way. Your job is to create a learning culture. Anyone who has led a team will tell you, culture is hard. Put thought and energy here, because for the creative team, the alternative is irrelevance.

PURGE THE TROLLS

"Have you ever seen a company or department paralyzed by someone who is unhappy and wants to take hostages? It is remarkable how much damage one person can do. If you haven't seen it, I suggest you watch "The Caine Mutiny." Basically, one guy takes apart the ship. He was unhappy. It only takes one."

- THE SECRET TO HAVING HAPPY EMPLOYEES. NYTIMES, 2010

"No brilliant jerks"

- REED HASTINGS

Team members who build fiefdoms walling others off from the company. Team members who spend their time trafficking in rumors from Glassdoor. Team members who manage to be at the center of every interpersonal outrage. Team members working against the team. Taking hostages, making demands.

In the parlance of James Collins in "Good to Great", some people are not on the bus. Office trolls come in the full high school portfolio of shapes and sizes. The human capacity for petty cruelty and destruction is staggering and it seems like every flavor eventually shows up in the workplace. It can't be completely helped. Given enough hires, transfers, promotions and time, some trolls, like weeds, are going to sprout.

In your role you must identify and remove them.

As a human being, your first instinct with a troublesome employee will be to talk to them, give them the benefit of the doubt, reason with them, and move beyond whatever the issue is. This is good, basic management. Someone who wants to be there will work with you, be honest with you, and let you know if the problem they have is something fixable. You have to listen, and be honest about if you can change whatever is making them unhappy. They have to accept it when you tell them a behavior needs to change. If you are both working in good faith, a lot of bad dynamics can turn around fast enough to give you whiplash.

If only it always went like this. There will be times when someone isn't being honest about why they are unhappy, or open about what they need to change. There will be times when you cannot and should not do the thing they want. Should you promote someone underserved who is acting out? Should you ignore the feedback on a star manager who belittles their employees and feels entitled to because of their talent? Should you keep an adequate but negative teammate who wants another job but hasn't motivated themselves to go get one?

For these and so many other toxic behaviors, no, you should not.

The trolls are easy to find because even with the light and energy of your sincere concern and attention, they won't change. They will read accommodation as weakness. Your attention as validation. They will look for advantage in manipulation.

Some people don't have good intentions. Some just want to watch the world burn.

This is one of those times when you have to divorce someone's craft skill from their behavior. Maybe they are good. Maybe very much so. There's simply no amount of craft one person can bring that makes up for damaging the team - and that is what is at risk. The rot goes deeper than you realize. Whatever problems you see are a taste of the ones they keep hidden from you. You're the boss. Their incentive is to hide their worst selves from you. If it's bad for you, it is much worse for everyone else.

Almost weekly the tech press share stories of founders being slow to fire star programmers, even when they drive others to misery. There's always a quote from the manager saying they were trying to be fair and describing how they hoped to work around the problem. These are teams embarking on a cultural death spiral. Read every article like this that you can find and file it away as a cautionary tale.

Keep your humanity. Give people an honest chance. But when they sprout, be decisive and purge the trolls.

DELEGATE
OWNERSHIP

"His coaching philosophy is, you're out there on the field, you can see the way the defense is lined up better than I can. So it's my job to get you to the best point believing in yourself and believing in your ability to call the plays. "

- CONNOR HALLIDAY QB, WASHINGTON ST. ABOUT COACH MIKE LEACH

E very team leader should have to spend a day playing Starcraft.

Starcraft is a famous real time strategy game, in which players build and lead a digital team - in this case an army of space marines - battling for control of a map. The player has a partial god-view of the goings on, with soldiers and workers skittering around, fighting and building things. The map is too big to take in all at once, and the unexplored areas are fogged over. Your virtual army responds to every command with snappy "Yes sir!"s and "Roger that"s before marching off to do what you told them. No one second guesses you. You have total control over the entire team.

As you play, you learn the challenge in real time strategy games is not strategy so much as managing your own attention. As more and more marines are added to the map the pace becomes overwhelming. You forget about parts of your army. You stop upgrading buildings on your base because you're busy launching attacks elsewhere. Factories sit idle because you haven't told them to produce anything.

You can do whatever you want with your team, but events are happening so fast you fall behind issuing orders. In Starcraft, it is not uncommon to find your base under attack, while your army stands around doing nothing because you haven't told them to fight back.

You have total control over all decision making, and you lose the game because of it.

This is the experience of working with disempowered teams. Assignments go out, teams work to complete them and when the work is done everyone sits around checking email, surfing the web or doing nothing at all until a more senior creative shows up to provide feedback or a new assignment. Your base is under attack. Your team is posting on Instagram. It's all your fault.

I'll stop torturing this metaphor.

This happens when the team is working against orders instead of goals. Outputs instead of outcomes. You have failed to delegate decision making so thoroughly that others won't decide. Or you have punished initiative when your team has shown it. Either way, you have a team that doesn't feel like it can move forward without you.

Every broken team I have ever worked with had in common that they would do nothing until they were told, and then do only what someone told them. They assumed anything done without direction would be thrown out and had learned not to waste their time. In fast moving professions, this is a disaster. Instead of dumb obedience, you need your team to see opportunities and to act on them without waiting for you. You need movement in the absence of direction.

The only way this will ever happen is if you delegate ownership for the work along with the work itself.

It turns out, this is hard to do. I find that creative leaders resist giving up control until they have no other choice. After all, if you aren't making the work, and you aren't making decisions about the work, then what would you say you do here?

This is misguided thinking. Beyond the fact that bottlenecking every decision with yourself doesn't scale, it also demotivates and devalues the best performers on your team. It's exactly the kind of control freak, older generation of management that has no business in the business of creativity. Instead of acting as a gatekeeper your job is to be an accelerant. Instead of rushing from one team to the next to deliver direction you should be experiencing a fire hose of inbound work and ideas you never asked for.

Working this way requires a lot of time explaining the whys and whats behind an assignment. Why are we doing this? What does success look like? What are the constraints? What else do we need to know about the context? You must explicitly tell the team that you expect them to make and own their own decisions.

Those decisions will be different than ones you would have made. Some of them are bound to be wrong. But giving up ownership is the only way to reach your team's true potential. Your metaphorical base will be under attack every day you have this job. Make sure your team knows you expect them to take the initiative fighting back.

WE'RE TALKING ABOUT PRACTICE, MAN

"No one's ever gotten better by practicing less."

– RON JAWORSKI

I have failed at few things as consistently as creating an ongoing training program. The need has always seemed obvious. If you want to get the most out of the team you hire, you need to put real effort into developing their talent beyond the limited scope of day to day work.

HR always seems to provide inadequate course supplements that go unused because they were bought and deployed without any input from the creative team. There is usually some kind of speaker series and it is usually not well attended. At every stop in my career, I have felt that if we were going to improve in a meaningful way, we were going to have to do more.

Over the years I have tried to roll my own supplemental training program and every time it's felt like the universe was lining up against me. First comes the money and the larger organizational support. Software companies like Google and MailChimp have the luxury of dedicated creative training budgets and the resulting programs like MailChimp University or Google's G2G reflect that. Companies in lower margin industries have a harder time approaching this by buying their way good.

Some of the specific quirks of agency life don't help. All companies face pressure to do more with less but few more than agencies. Client fire drills abound, and the billable hour looms large. As a year goes by, the always tiny training budget slips away to fund moral building or goodbye drinks. What remains is a subscription to Lynda.com (If you are reading this and ever learned something there please @ me) and learning on the job from your peer set.

Then there are the cultural problems. Training and practice seems to highlight and even exaggerate team fissures. It brings out the back of the class child cynic in us. Don't like that team member's design? You will definitely have some snark for the talk they lead. Regional differences and technology problems also feel amplified. One of my homespun programs tried having craft experts give half hour tutorials on a national stage via video conference and failed so badly I had to promise my team to never bring it back. We postponed another because of scheduling conflicts for so long that it died when the person leading it finally left the company.

In all this failure there were some high points. On a team that was slow to execute work, we drilled shortcut keys in timed races, posting the best times on a shared leaderboard. The game became so competitive that a long running and heated argument broke out on whether ADD meds should be considered performance enhancing drugs. On several teams, training took the form of brew and view sessions, where teams watched award submission videos from various shows over beers and debated whether they deserved the accolades.

Absent a confident one size fits all approach to training (spend money?) I can still offer thoughts on things that have worked better or worse. In that spirit and with humility, I offer the following suggestions for planning a team training. Nothing guarantees success, but some failures are avoidable.

Delegate With Care

Not everyone is the right person to lead a training and those not right people have a weird way of being the first to volunteer. You should only be choosing teammates who others already respect, and you should be making it clear it's a vote of confidence for them, not a punishment. Find a way to block the not-right folks, or risk unintentionally elevating a low performer and turning off the team.

Minimize Prep

Lesson plans and presentation materials are time sucks to create. If you ever want to feel sympathy for a teacher, try to come up with thirty minutes of material to interest your smartest peers. The best training finds ways to get a lot out of a little bit of setup.

Design for Fun

Few of us really enjoyed school so should feel no pressure to recreate it. If you can't think of a way to make what you are trying to train fun, you shouldn't bother. So much of work is work, you can't get people to take part in something, lean forward and learn if it feels like more drudgery.

Cadence Matters

Training or practice sessions are a habit that need repetition to work but enough space not to be a burden. If you are doing them once a year, don't expect a skill lift from them. If you do them weekly, lesson quality sags and attendance falls off. There isn't a magic number for frequency, so strive for the Goldilox feeling of good content, attendance and engagement.

Self Directed Training - a panacea?

The most successful low-budget training approach I have found, by far, is to supplement and fuel the sort of self-directed learning creatives undertake on their own. In some ways the whole idea of a shared session has become an anachronism. With free, instant access to nearly infinite content on any niche topic imaginable, gathering as a group to learn from an imperfect instructor might be a romantic relic we don't need anymore.

For a long time I've noticed the most avid learners on my teams were ripping through YouTube how-tos at 2X speed on their own time. Self motivated learners can pick up more tool tricks in an hour on TikTok, and at better production value, than in a year of meetings, coursework or conferences. Why not embrace a professional Montessori model and let the team do it on their own time?

I called my take on this 1% Better. The idea is to add a little bit of structure to self-directed learning by asking the team to declare what they plan to learn (anything they felt would help with their job), and then have every team member share back their progress in a short (ten minutes or less) presentation. We scheduled the presentations in blocks of three or four, called "Demo days".

On their own time, team members made AR prototypes and experimented with Lottie. They went deep on design systems and researched generative copywriting tools. And the Demo Days were fun. Knowing they were presenting to their peers, team members worked hard on their presentations, trying to outdo one another with quality, comedy and inspired work. It was not perfect, but it was far better than anything else I have tried.

Practice and training are tough to take seriously, but no one gets better by practicing less. If you're looking for a format that works for your team, try this one.

The Brief: Get 1% Better
Pick literally any skill or subject at any altitude that you want to

learn more about, and in a self directed way, improve that skill over the course of the next month.

A month from now, the team will come back together for demo day and share what we learned.

Each team member will present back the one thing they learned, how they learned it, and what everyone should know about it, for ten minutes.

LEADING WITH A
GM MINDSET

"Guys, you're still trying to replace Giambi. I told you we can't do it, and we can't do it. Now, what we might be able to do is recreate him. Recreate him in the aggregate."

- BILLY BEANE, MONEYBALL

I f you woke up today and the Finance director told you your team had an extra $200K to spend on salary, what would you do? Would you rather use it to hire three entry level creatives or a tenured Creative Director? Or would you use the money to promote several of your star teammates and lessen the chance of their job hunting? Or maybe you would like to make one mid level hire and to keep the remaining money available to give you flexibility later on? Or make a hire or two that would give your team new capabilities?

It's fun to think about. Extra salary unlocks so much possibility.

Now pretend you woke up today and one of your Creative Directors quit. What would you do? If you're anything like the majority of creative leaders, you would head to recruiting and get a candidate search going for a new Creative Director. This is missing an opportunity, and it's one of the most important lessons you can learn as you grow and shape your team.

You may or may not have access to it, but beneath the titles and the levels, buried in a spreadsheet or business plan somewhere, there is an amount that your company wants to spend on your team's total compensation. This is your salary cap. Your goal is to stop planning and having conversations through an assumed set of individual roles, and start planning in terms of what the highest quality team is that you can buy for your cap number.

This means being thoughtful about skill sets, levels, structure and work volume. It means thinking through trade-offs around what work needs full time employees, and what can be done as needed using freelancers. It means that when a Creative Director quits, you ask the question, *what is the best use of the salary this frees up?* before you go running to recruiting.

When you think in terms of salary cap instead of roles, every team departure is an opportunity to promote from within. To add capabilities. To fix the compensation for underpaid stars. And to add junior staff. Cap space is a chance to restructure and rethink. It is the ultimate control to design the team as you want it to be.

You can be forgiven if this isn't how you were trained to see the world. In most organizations, getting to a cap approach is harder than it should be. Salary falls under the accounting bucket called Operating Expenditures (OpEx) and is monitored and controlled by your Finance team and guarded by Human Resources. Neither tend to be forthcoming about it at an individual or team level. Managing through a salary cap requires partnering with both capabilities. You will have to explain yourself, and win them over to having conversations about what's possible in the numbers instead of sitting at the kids table and trying to guess what they will allow.

If your experience is anything like mine, this will be a painful, touchy, often circular set of conversations. You will be treading where you are unwelcome. Until someone takes you seriously, you should expect to be warned away, told you don't understand how this works or both.

But the upside is worth it. The next time someone leaves your team, instead of feeling the loss, you will be asking questions about the right thing. What does this make possible?

DE-RISK BIG HIRES

I have a vivid memory of drinking bourbon out of coffee cups, late on a friday night with my office mate (the ACDs had shared, two person offices back then). We were taking a break from pitch work to read the hire announcement emails. You know the emails - they're the ones that go around after a big hire, listing their awarded campaigns and the famous brands they shaped before joining. All their big named stops. There are links to the announcement PR put out to the trades. Maybe an interview somewhere. A reference to their sneaker collection.

I have a vivid memory of us doing dramatic bourbon infused re-readings one Friday night. Not one of these stars was still with the company.

I couldn't tell you exactly when I noticed that the senior hires were failing a lot, but once I did I couldn't unsee it. It was more noticeable because there were so many fewer of those roles. It was more noticeable because every time one turned over, it caused so much more team damage. It got so bad that my office mate and I started keeping an informal dead-pool of creative VPs - trying to guess the month they would be gone.

Leadership churn does funny things to a company. Our senior creatives were washing out so often that it stopped mattering to the teams who leadership was. Pressed to do something new or different, they learned to ignore the latest star hire and wait for the next one. In the gaps, team leaders emerged, won their peers' respect and were passed over in favor of new big hires, before quitting in frustration.

On more than one occasion, we'd gone from a big time, team-leading hire to a full-team reboot in a quarter. I'm sure there are many reasons stars stop being stars after a job change, but one uncomfortable one is this; talent isn't as portable as you think it is.

In "The Numbers Game", author Chris Anderson's exploration of data in soccer, he describes the common phenomenon of soccer clubs hiring a star player whose star fades after the move. Anderson writes, "The idea that ability is encapsulated within an individual, and so can easily be moved around, bought and sold" is itself a mistake. A 2006 article in Harvard Business Review goes further, arguing, "You never know whether an assortment of stars will work together effectively once they are separated from the conditions and resources that made them successful in previous environments. Star performers don't operate in a vacuum; they operate as part of a team, and their success stems at least in part from their team relationships."

The high-scorer on the soccer pitch is a product of the system, the competition and the mid-fielders creating chances. The award winning Creative Director is a product of her team, the company culture of excellence, the department brand that buoys her recommendations and the good taste level of her clients. Context makes the hero.

I find that this idea runs so counter to how most people think that many feel personally attacked by it. Noone wants to hear that success is dependent on things outside themselves. Whether it makes you comfortable or not, If you are about to make a big hire you should have it top of mind, because while you can be confident that a star candidate has been successful before, you cannot know what parts of their success they're bringing with them. This ambiguity attaches outsized risk to any big hire.

Since you can't and shouldn't avoid making the best hires possible, you have to do everything in your power to de-risk them.

Promote first

Better not to make this hire at all if you can avoid it. When a spot opens on your team, start your search by checking every possible internal candidate before looking outside. Check your roster for a team member who, when given time and attention, can grow into the role. Can you imagine them getting there in the next year? If you can, promote. The morale boost and cultural continuity of investing in your own people pays dividends.

Make more big hires

The same HBR article lamenting the struggles of star hires in new contexts proposes a solution; bring the old context with them. Dubbed the "lift-out", authors Groysberg and Abrahams argue that hiring the star's team as well as the star makes their success more likely. If you are trying to de-risk cultural disorientation, it might help to go big.

Nerf the team

If you passed someone over for the role, move them to a different team before you onboard your big hire. There's no reason to tempt fate by having a good but not good enough to promote team member waiting for your star to arrive. Whatever they say, they will be feeling burned by not getting promoted. They will be skeptical of the new hire. If they become vindictive, they are well positioned to cause lasting dysfunction. I recognize this is cynical, but I have seen it happen enough times to assume the worst and pre-empt it.

Overmanage, at first

The tendency I see most often after making a big creative hire is to be hands off and let them do their thing. No one successful wants to find out the hard way they made a move under a micromanaging boss. While this is well intentioned, it leaves too much to chance, especially in the first weeks and months. As the creative leader, you have to set the tone for how your new star will engage, respond to feedback and collaborate. The best way to do that is by being present and engaged.

Avoid Sunk Cost fallacy

Even if you do everything right, this can go wrong. Sometimes the body rejects the organ. Too many creative leaders, having passed over an internal candidate to interview, hire, and onboard a new one, then refuse to see their mistake. They wrote that loving welcome email. It can be very hard to take it back.

If your new star player is failing, the only thing left is mitigation. Don't make it worse by doubling down on a mistake. Be out front of saying it didn't work, and move the team on to plan B.

There will be times when you have to make important hires as part of leading a creative team. Few things can be as damaging as the wrong one. Be systemic about the risks and remember, context makes the hero.

WHY INTERVIEW
CREATIVES

Whether they're short or long, group or individual, job interviews are a flawed, misleading and only marginally helpful way of finding out anything about a candidate. Handshakes, eye contact and follow up notes all seem to matter about as much as tarot cards as indicators of future success. As Yale professor Jason Dana put it in his the-title-is-the-plot New York Times piece The Utter Uselessness of Job Interviews, "Interviewers typically form strong but unwarranted impressions about interviewees, often revealing more about themselves than the candidates." Amen.

There is only so much you can learn about someone in an hour or less when their only motivation is to make you like them and want to work with them. After years of trying different approaches to improve our interviews, I came to a bit of a realization.

By the time I interview someone, I have usually spent enough time with their portfolio to feel very good about whether they could be a useful part of our team. For years I found that our hit rate finding good freelancers was better than when we hired mid to senior-level full-time employees. This was surprising because we often weren't interviewing the freelancers at all. The nature of the needs meant that by the time we got a freelancer role approved, we were getting desperate for their help. If we liked their book, they were in and if they didn't work out, we could end the contract a couple weeks later. But somehow, these less vetted candidates ended up sticking around. People nobody had spoken to apart from an HR conversation confirming their rate and start date were succeeding where vetted candidates were not.

Reflecting on this, it might be a quirk unique to the creative team. In this job, the old BBDO-ism applies - it's about the work the work the work. The rounds of interviews you are having are time wasted churning up unhelpful data. Who honestly cares what someone says in an awkward thirty minute 1:1 in some forgotten mini conference room when they have a strong portfolio highlighting years of work and great references? Not me. Not anymore anyway.

I have not been successful at dumping interviews completely. The tradition runs deep, the suggestion of abandoning it is seen as reckless, and even now I have to go through the motion of bleeding this patient. So if, like me, you accept that there is only a very limited amount to learn from a job interview, what is it that you should be trying to learn?

Interview or Sell?

Some candidates are less sure about you than you are of them. Maybe they aren't looking that hard for their next stop. Or maybe the hot takes on Glassdoor stuck with them. Whatever it is, try to get a sense early on if you should be selling them on the role as you are vetting them. A lot of interviewers assume they are on the power side of that dynamic only to get turned down by an unimpressed candidate once they make an offer.

Improv - Ability

Years ago I interviewed for a senior role at Riot Games (I didn't get it). Late in the process, I interviewed with Tom Cadwell - The Design Director of League of Legends and creator of World of Warcraft. The recruiter managing the process gave me a little bit of preparation for each round of interviews but for Tom he seemed equal parts concerned and lost for what to tell me. Tom had a reputation for being difficult and the recruiter was insistent that I understood that.

When I spoke to Tom I found him anything but. Smart and funny, he spent the first few minutes doing the normal getting-to-know-you stuff before getting into the conversation that he wanted to have. Tom asked me what the last game was that addicted me and I told him it was a mobile game called World of Tanks I used to kill time on my commute. For a founder of the largest E-Sports concern going, I'm sure this answer ranked up there with Pac Man, but at least he was familiar with it, laughed and moved on to what I enjoyed and what I didn't about the game. As we talked it came out that Tom and I agreed the game could use some improvement with what happened to your character after you died. WOT is a team-based shooter format, and once your character is dead, you turn into a spectator. You can watch the rest of the game to see if your team wins but there's nothing else to keep you engaged. Tom asked if he tasked me with designing World of Tanks to improve the game for people who had been eliminated, what would I do? What followed was 40 minutes of him and I riffing together on all the different ways that you could make a losing player still feel engaged without ruining the game play for everyone else.

I've thought a lot about that interview. The conversation we had told Tom a lot more about who I was and how I thought than any directed interview questions would have. It was a wild, ranging, punchy and fun conversation. I can't imagine anything starting with, "Tell me about a time you...." having been even close to as worthwhile. Tom understood the role he was filling was a creative one, and what he wanted to see, even in a limited way, was whether I could create something. How I would generate ideas. What questions I would ask. How easily I could come up with interesting or provocative approaches, discard them and move on to new ones. I have used a version of Tom's approach when interviewing candidates ever since.

When I do this with candidates I'm less interested in solution quality than quantity, and less interested in problem fluency than attitude. Do they lean into trying to solve something with limited information or do they recoil and search for an excuse to not try? It's amazing how many people with great resumes reject a blank sheet of paper when it's put in front of them. On the flip side, it's invigorating to walk out of a conversation with someone who spins your head with possibilities for how you might approach something. That's something you don't learn from a portfolio and it's someone you should hire.

Presentation Ability

Making the work is so completely different from being able to talk about it that it can be like speaking two different languages. If the role you're interviewing for requires someone to be able to convince as well as create, interviews are the perfect time to find out if they can. This can be as simple as asking a candidate to walk through the thought process behind a piece in their portfolio or as rigorous as asking them to prepare a presentation on something ahead of time. For a long time certain teams at R/GA required every candidate from ACD up to give a half hour presentation to the team they were interviewing with.

Like improv ability, presentation ability is something very very difficult to fake. You may not know if they are any good as a creative but you will know if you can put them in front of a stakeholder and have them tell a coherent story.

Depth and Range

The last thing you can reliably get from a job interview is the one thing unstructured interviews tend to be good at finding out - whether the candidate has any depth or range of interest. What are their hobbies? What are they reading? What are they doing when they're not doing this? Does it sound like they have any idea what's happening in the world? Are they attached to or passionate about any subcultures? Do they have a side hustle? Are they makers on any media platforms?

This isn't without controversy. An argument can be made (and often is on social media) that this stuff has nothing to do with the job, isn't on the job description, isn't any of the employer's business and therefor shouldn't be part of the process. I find this flawed in the same way job descriptions are. You are hiring for intangibles as much as you are hiring for a list of discrete skills. Candidates who don't want this to matter aren't being honest about the dynamic nature of this work.

Candidates who don't show curiosity, who don't have any hobbies or interests, aren't going to be great cultural adds to your team. They aren't going to have the range of esoteric, bizarre and niche influences that you don't know you need yet, so they're going to be waiting around for someone else to tell them what's actually happening in the world or what's interesting to other people. They have great technical skills and nothing else.

A creative team needs some weird to function. It needs a reservoir of things you never know to ask for to appear at the right time in the right place on the right briefs. It doesn't matter what the specific interests of a candidate are, what their hobbies are or what they waste their weekends on; it only matters that these aren't blanks.

AWARDS AND SPEC

Award and spec work deserve extra scrutiny when recruiting for different versions of the same reason; each is a false signal of quality.

Complaining about spec work in portfolios is trendy. The argument is that since the work wasn't produced, of course it's good. It never had to contend with clients or technological limitations. It never met reality. Show me something good that went live and I can tell you if a candidate has any real talent. Ideas not made real belong in college portfolios, or worse, on Dribbble.

There's a bitterness to these arguments. The unspoken sentence of, "I could have done that if not for my client / account lead / tech team / budget / media buy " is implicit.

There is also an implied knock on quality. If the thinking or execution weren't good, that would be the criticism. Instead, for some reason we are supposed to be annoyed that a candidate presented work they are proud of without the backing of a public reaction or plate of awards and without the support of the other capabilities at their last job propping it up.

I have always liked spec work and found it strange that creative leads, who spend their days critting work that isn't live, suddenly become disdainful of it when they are recruiting. The candidate is showing a pure representation of their ability and bar for quality.

Why should you care if the rest of their team wasn't able to build it or sell it in? You don't know if it would have worked in-market, only whether you like it. Take it for the pure creative exercise that it is and weigh it on its merits.

Awarded work is the mirror image. Seeking candidates who have award winning work is a staple shorthand of creative recruiting. Unable to judge the quality of a portfolio, we grab on to the certified opinions of others. Job postings ask for listings of awards won, and recruiters themselves stake out award banquets, handing business cards to the winners. None of us believes nine out of ten dentists recommend that toothpaste but for some reason we lose our own judgment at first sight of an industry trophy on a resume.

When recruiting a heavily awarded candidate, ignore the accolades and focus on their role in the work. This is a team sport - their winning campaign was the product of a lot of people, opportunities and circumstances - and you won't be hiring any of that. Awards given for the totality of work mean next to nothing about an individual's contribution. Often the teams who touch the most awarded pieces number in the dozens. Anyone who has ever served on a creative jury can tell you how bizarre and fickle the process for selecting winners is.

There are years where it feels like every candidate for a position somehow has the same famous piece of work in their book. One year everyone had Nike+. Another year everyone had Small Business Saturday. What did they all do on those projects? Maybe something. Maybe something important. It's hard to say. Among the thousand parents that success had, someone must have made it, but the odds that their portfolio is the one that found your inbox are longer than you think.

UNBOX THE ONBOARDING EXPERIENCE

"Hire with care but integrate deliberately and fast"

-BORIS GROYSBERG

You know the feeling. You bought the new car / couch / stereo / house / whatever and you can't stop playing with it. You tell your friends about all the features and the things you can do now that you couldn't before. Your life is different for having this thing. Better for it. You wallow in the afterglow of having spent the money (an investment!) and learn every little talking point you can find about how it's made and what it is capable of. Two weeks later it's like it never happened. Reality found equilibrium. The universe righted itself. You wouldn't admit it to anyone, but this new world is a new normal, and normal isn't ever that great.

That's how your new hire feels about this job. A narrow window of pins and needles and optimism and bragging followed by the inevitable grind of a co-worker they don't like on an assignment that's beneath them. There's a window, for our purposes, we're going to say a four week window, when they are really and truly excited to be here. That window is going to close. The shiny new feeling will fade. And cultural integration is going to get much, much harder.

Onboarding happens whether or not your company puts effort into it - it just becomes a function of the Finance, IT and HR teams. Try to tell me with a straight face you would trust any of them to make someone feel good about something. They onboard with rules. With passwords. With legalese and training modules about spearfishing attacks. They have the vaguest, thinnest idea of what you and your team does, and in the first few hours of your recruits tenure, they seem determined to prove it

A colleague once described their first day as a meeting about filling out timesheets followed by a low quality public service announcement about oversharing on social media being a career risk. Inspiring stuff. At one of my stops, a senior design hire from Nike was so put off by the lackluster onboarding that he nearly quit hours into the first day of work. Like a lot of first impressions, the early hours and days a team member spends with you are determinate of what they will think of you later on. You need to take aggressive control of this time.

There is a right and a wrong way to do this. The right way is to have a plan. To have materials and the people ready. To have thought about everything you could possibly want to indoctrinate someone with and to have it in an entertaining format. This is a multi-channel campaign to remind a talented person that they made the right decision when they joined your team. Spare no expense. Scrutinize the experience of them arriving at their desk for the first time. Humanize the corporate parts. Give them as many reminders as you can about who you are and what you value. Keep the information coming and follow it all up when they are settled in by asking for feedback about what else you could have done.

Some companies have this figured out and you can learn a lot studying them. Riot Games famously puts new hires through a week-long De-Noobification to get them deep in the culture. Facebook's employee handbook, "Facebook Was Not Created to be a Company" is an incredible statement of values grafted onto a meditation about their work and industry. Photos of the swag and welcome notes that greet new team members at employee-minded companies are everywhere on social media.

Onboarding a team members is an investment as important as finding them in the first place. Put in the time it takes to make it memorable. Even if you don't, your new hire will remember.

NUANCE AND FREELANCERS

F reelance contract workers are so pervasive in the creative industry that they make up a stable majority of some teams. Over half of Google's employee roster is reportedly contract employees. I haven't worked on a creative team in over a decade that wasn't at least 10% freelance. As the nature of our work changes driven by cost and geographic pressures, we can expect more, not less, of a move towards these roles. In your role, you should be familiar with some of the quirky advantages and disadvantages that come with this work arrangement. On a surface level, a freelancer is like any other team member. You hired them for a certain role or skill set, you add them to the team and they do the job like anyone else.

That surface similarity belies some pretty serious differences underpinning the whole nature of their contribution. Most obvious is that, for whatever reason, they are temporary team members (you could argue that everyone is a temporary team member - but some are more so). Freelancers join teams through some combination of companies limiting payroll, and the freelancers wanting independence and flexibility . The company can cut costs in minutes by telling freelancers not to come to work the next day - contract over. No severance, no HR required. Freelancers can look ahead to their next assignment, and if it's looking boring they can skip to another more interesting or better paying gig. No two weeks notice. No awkward resignation meeting.

In practice, this leads to some pretty strange team dynamics. Perceiving them as temporary, companies avoid investing time or resources in their success. It's not uncommon for them to join with no onboarding, have no line managers and get no formal career feedback. They aren't invited to the Christmas party or the team off-site. They aren't given the company swag. Great contractors tend to get their contracts extended and stick around for a while. That will make it all the more awkward when consciously or otherwise they end up treated as a class apart.

There are other downsides. Full-time team members are usually aware that Freelancers are hourly employees. When a team is grinding out late nights, the freelancer is getting compensated time and a half while your permanent employees are watching their lives fritter away. Because they signed on for a temporary arrangement, freelancers can decide they would rather not do the boring work, and some managers will respond by assigning it to the full-time employees so as not to risk scaring away strong mercenary talent.

If not managed well, this creates a strange professional caste system, with different flavors of resentment and bad feedback loops baked in. So what to do? Experience says this is another moment when you should remind yourself that finance is not your problem. Having a well compensated underclass kicking around does not make the work better, so in as much as possible you should try to treat contract employees as employees. Invite them to the company town hall and the training, and let them bill for it. Give them the stupid t-shirt and notebook.

While leading Creative at the ORGANIC agency I tried to make this shift happen, right down to a freelance-centric (benefits free) version of our onboarding. During my tenure I personally recruited and referred around three quarters of our freelance talent from my network. Our small scale made it easier - I nearly had enough professional acquaintances, former teammates and friends to fill our needs - but fissures existed and I'm still looking for a model that recognizes the human reality of contract vs FTE work and does a good job of blending both in a single company.

Our welcome note (included below) is a flavor of the culture we tried to create with contract workers on the creative team, even in the absence of a supportive financial structure.

> Freelancer, contractor, remote worker, part-timer. This industry seems to need a lot of labels to be comfortable with the dynamic way people live their lives.
>
> We don't.
>
> Nothing is forever. Some people come for a career, others for a couple of days. Either way, we're excited you signed up.
>
> For however long you're here, you're one of us. Speak up. Dig in. Make the work and the people around you better. Learn some new tricks and teach us a few.
>
> If your next stop isn't with us we hope you leave with work you want in your portfolio and a bigger network of talented people you want to work with. We hope you stay in touch, because we plan to.
>
> Welcome to the team.
>
> -Carlson

DON'T COUNTER

People get other job offers. It can feel like the second you get everyone on the same page, you're ahead of the work and starting to groove that the recruiters start calling. In the agency and technology worlds, talent raids are a fact of life. The tables at advertising award shows are paid partly out of recruiting budgets. Headhunters patrol the bar looking for creatives who's salary doesn't yet match the hardware they just won. As soon as you have a team worth knowing, they are going to start getting calls.

It's a matter of time before one of your stars resigns for some other place offering a bigger title and a twenty percent raise. Your mind will race to how to break the news to the clients who adore them or the team that they carry. You ask if they are sure about their decision. You tell them not to accept the offer and ask how long you have before they do. And right after this talk, you hustle to the HR lead and start figuring out what you can do for a counter offer. Talented people are the difference between success and failure so it's no wonder the default setting is to do whatever you can to hang onto them.

It shouldn't be.

Only about half of those who receive a counter offer accept it and a full ninety three percent leave within eighteen months. Counter offers tend to paper over whatever frustrations lead to someone choosing to leave in the first place. If they accept your counter, they aren't staying. They just haven't left yet.

Further, quitting to receive a counter offer has long been a career accelerator in competitive talent markets. It is a de facto promotion. Once you start giving into this as a reason to advance someone's career, your promotion criteria are meaningless. The rest of the team will find out what happened - no matter who you swear to secrecy - and the damage will spread. Others will entertain offers as a path to career advancement. This is a feedback loop that's best avoided in the first place.

Is countering always bad? No, but understand it for what it is. If you need to buy time to get a succession plan in place or a team in order, roll the dice. If you can use it as a way of forcing a deserved promotion, consider it. But make sure to make it rare, and be clear eyed about the odds of it working out.

People get other job offers. Sometimes they take them. The world doesn't end. Nothing says more about the health of your team than the message that no one is irreplaceable.

FIRING SOMEONE

"Would you rather get one shot in the head or five in the chest and bleed to death?"
"Are those my only options? "

BILLY BEANE AND PETER BRAND, MONEYBALL

If you lead a team, you will eventually have to let go of a team member. As soon as you realize someone isn't going to work out, you need to begin the process. Procrastinating hurts your credibility with the rest of your team while demotivating everyone picking up the slack. It becomes a cosmic drag on work while the best team members question your commitment to quality. As James Collins put it in Good to Great, "Letting the wrong people hang around is unfair to the right people."

That clarity doesn't make it easy.

The Silicon Valley notion that you are setting someone free to do something that better fits their skillset is optimistic at best. If you know your team well, and you should, you will know what their career hopes are, whether they are buying a home or planning a wedding. You will know what the job market is doing and have a good sense of how soon they are likely to get a new one. If you are in the US, you also know what this does for their access to our dystopian healthcare system. You are not blind. Don't lie to yourself about what this is. You might be "freeing them" from the expectations of a job that isn't the right fit but you are also throwing them into the deep end of the uncertainty pool. Your challenge is to do the right thing, but with the most humanity possible.

There are two ways through this that I've encountered. The first is to work with your HR department to make sure that you're giving a fired employee the most generous package possible. It's not unusual for long tenured employees to get several weeks or even months of severance pay as part of an exit, and like everything else, it is negotiable. A good manager will advocate for as much as you can get on their behalf, even as you are working to move them on their way.

The second approach requires having a real relationship with the team member and trusting them not to turn against you and the team. If you have to cut someone you trust, try what former investoPedia CEO David Siegel called a "transparent separation".

"With transparent separations, you don't blindside an underperforming employee or fire him outright. Instead, you encourage him to leave on his own by letting him know he is going to be let go in time and needs to start looking for a new job ASAP."

This is an honest way to approach a bad job fit, and maximizes the chances of someone finding something better and leaving on their own terms. It's always easiest to find a job when you already have one. Use that dynamic to help this person on their way.

Whether you use a generous package or a transparent separation, it's important not to procrastinate when a team member isn't working out. In twenty years of New York advertising - not a business for the squeamish - I can hardly think of an instance where a manager was too quick to cut an under-performing teammate. Instead, the most common and frustrating truth is that even the people that are trying to be tyrants tend to be decent human beings. The ones who want to be liked will go to absurd lengths to avoid firing someone. This is a huge mistake. As soon as you know someone isn't working out, pick your path, swallow hard and do what's right for the team.

THE ALUMNI
NETWORK

"I've come around to the idea that this is going to be more like an NCAA basketball team than a family."

- RICH BLOOM, HUGE INC.

"When they depart, they will go with the best wishes of the club, and then the whole system will start again."

- AT AJAX, ONE STAR GOES, ANOTHER IS GOING, AND MORE ARE ALWAYS COMING, NYTIMES

C reative work is filled with opinionated, skeptical, striving people in mixes of focus and distraction. Certainty and doubt. Dedication and flight. Something about the job makes short tenures normal as a transient troupe of makers job hops, for project, client and role variety as much as for anything that looks like career opportunity. It is common for hiring managers to see creatives who have stayed somewhere more than a few years as somehow damaged. If they're so good, why did they stick around?

There are no company lifers. Even if your teammates like you, like working for you (not the same thing), like your company, like the work they are doing and the people they do it with, they are still going to leave you. Their feet will itch. They will hear The New calling. And you will have to replace them. If you are good at recruiting and putting people in places to succeed, you will have more deserving team members than you can promote anyway. The ones who leave are preventing a career logjam. Stars leaving for bigger roles elsewhere make room for the next group.

Which is all fine and good in theory but can be impossible to remember the moment one of your favorites give notice. While your head is spinning asking why they quit and calculating the knock on damage to the work and the team, you are liable to get emotional. To take the exit personally. You weren't a bad boss (if you're reading this you're at least trying right?) but even if you were, you are a much worse one if you use the moment someone exits to be petty, trash talk them, ghost them or do any of the other childish things people do when hurt. Acting out is going to alienate your teammate and everyone else. People will already be upset by the departure of a favorite. Pettiness in leadership makes it worse.

Yes an exit is at least a partial rejection of you - someone on your team decided they would be happier in another place with other people doing other things - but it's less about you than you think. If it's a normal, drama-free on-to-the-next-one quitting, you should be fawning over them, reminding everyone how great they have been, planning going away activities and working with them on a smooth transition. Teammates should be leaving feeling good about what they left behind and the decision they made.

If you can get yourself into this headspace, there is at least one big upside in every star departure; the chance to learn something.

Your departed will be meeting a whole new group of people and some of them will be impressive. Some of them will even be looking for new opportunities.

In, "The Alliance; Managing Talent in the Networked Age", LinkedIn CEO Reid Hoffman calls this "Network Intelligence", where every former employee becomes a potential source of information, while you remain a source of opportunity and information for them. This strikes me as a pretty high concept way of saying it's smart to keep up with people you like working with. Whatever you call it, being proactive about touching base with alumni is about the best recruiting and trend spotting tool you have. It's also easy to neglect it thinking about networking for your own next stop instead as a way to build your current one.

I have found ex-teammates to be an incredible source of information on emerging tools and techniques. On companies crashing or hitting their stride. And on talent. They are often my first stop when hiring because they have a much more intimate understanding of what I am looking for in recruits, and there isn't any confusion about quality. I get notes all the time from alumni saying I should look at this or that person's portfolio who is job hunting. Just as often, I get notes from peers and former teammates asking if I can recommend someone with a certain skill set.

Losing a valued team member is never easy. Whatever it takes for you to get there, you have to be happy for them. It should help to remind yourself that even as they are at another company, they are still helping you by building out your alumni network.

3 SYSTEMS

Maximize your own time by being deliberate about the things competing for it. Experience says there will be three buckets, each with their own nuances, where effort put into organization will pay returns in time and control later on. These three buckets are, general tasks (Productivity), consumption of creative fuel (Knowledge) and recruitment, deployment and growth of team members (Network). You should be working through a systemic approach for each.

Systems need some habit discipline to work, but like your 401K, they grow exponentially in value over time. A productivity system manages the competing demands that come with growing responsibilities. A knowledge system acts as a personal database of professional experience and best practices - hot starting your teams and work product. A network system frees you to tap into creative talent without intermediaries who don't understand it as intimately as yourself.

With each, a small amount of ongoing care and feeding sets you up for big returns as a creative lead.

THE PRODUCTIVITY
SYSTEM

I t is possible, even likely, to reach a creative leadership role without great organizational skills. Superlative work can be made in spite of shambolic processes, and today's digital tools mean small teams requiring less coordination can have outsized impacts. It is possible for brute force to overcome inefficiency. To offload organization to project management or push through logistics failures. Grinding hours can make up for poor planning. It is possible for the unorganized to win.

But it will not scale. Your time will run out. Your ability to will things into being will fail. Your inbox will be both full and unread. Deadlines and details will begin to slip and quality with them. Whether you break down at two projects or ten, three team members or thirty, at some point if you don't have a formal way of organizing, you will break down. Winging it doesn't work in leadership.

Having a good productivity system is like being a designer with a well organized source file. You have a god-view of what needs to be done and a way to prioritize the doing. Instead of reacting to events, you are orchestrating them.

Productivity systems are the fad diets of knowledge workers.

There will always be a new one someone industry-famous swears by, but in the same way the best camera is the one you have with you, the best productivity system is the one you use as a habit.

You may try to invent your own way through this. That would be a mistake. What got you here probably wasn't about efficiency. Learn from someone who has spent more time than you ever will figuring this out. Read their book, watch their video, use their system and move on.

Over the years I have tried many, and found these to be the best combination of effort to pay off. Pick one, pick a notebook or tool to support it, and make it part of your professional routine.

- **Zen to Done:** A light, tool agnostic system of to-do lists and routines from Leo Baubauta.

- **Bullet Journaling:** An analog system of task tracking and prioritization from Ryder Caroll.

- **Kanban:** You may be more familiar with Kanban as a project management system than a productivity one, but the same simplified organization of To-Do, Doing, Done can be applied to yourself.

- **Time Blocking:** A system that combines to-do lists with assigning periods throughout the day for completion of specific tasks.

THE KNOWLEDGE
SYSTEM

An enormous corpus of adjacent work exists outside of the creative product you are responsible for. There are frameworks and presentation formats. Business-famous quotes and models of human behavior. There are so many damn brand houses.

As you advance, larger parts of your time will be taken up by strategy and communications. Both are critical to getting your work approved and made - and both will fall more on you than you think. And as unimpressive as those models, facts and frameworks sometimes are, they are an incredible time-sucking distraction to invent from scratch, under deadline, when you ought to be focusing on the creative product.

The second system for maximizing your time is a knowledge system - a plan for cataloging all these useful scraps of intellectual property you collect over your career, with the goal of re-using as much as humanly possible. A good knowledge system is the difference between "we need a slide sort of like this" and googling for that stat you heard three months ago but can't source at two in the morning. It is the choice between excellent frameworks you have seen used with success, and heated metaphysical debates about what a framework even is. A good system will maximize the amount of high quality content you are taking in and minimize the time it takes to recall or reference any of it.

My own is a drive with complete presentations I want to reference, paired with a google deck of loose slides organized as follows;

- **Frameworks:** High level ways of organizing problems. This is the home of the brand houses, customer journeys, behavior models and other abstractions found in strategy decks and business books.

- **Facts**: There is a limit to the number of times you can google and source the perfect stat about Millenials ignoring advertising before losing your grip. Do it once, add it here, and update it when it feels old.

- **Observations**: Observations are tricky because they are neither absolute enough to be facts or secret or refined enough to work as an insight. Over the years I have found this to be the most fruitful bucket when making the case for creativity, as it's a way of parking and referring to things that feel true but that are not supported with data. " "Pre-existing Condition" is a capitalist way of saying "Medical History"" is an interesting observation about our healthcare system. "Every Web3 brand has to use the Monument Sans font" is a great one about design in 2021. Neither on their own is of much value, but as part of a larger case about people, trends and attitudes, observations are very valuable. Observations also aren't something you can search out at the last minute. When you have one, or happen onto one, there is a real benefit to taking the time to document it so it's there when you need it.

- **Insights:** An insight is an unexpected truth that confers a competitive advantage. Insights are rare and not easily generalized. They also expire as they become widely known.

If you happen onto one or have one, save it and act on it before it spoils.

Any scrap of IP that interests me gets added to my knowledge system. Sometimes I remove things that have aged out of relevance. Once in a while I flip through it all as a refresher of what's there. It is the accumulation of thousands of presentations, clients, verticals, competitive reviews, projects and other professionals thinking. It's a lot.

When I step into a project, I go through my normal creative process, but instead of starting cold, I'm beginning from the cumulative thinking of years spent cataloging and evaluating. I'm choosing from IP to build from or recognizing the problem is of a different sort. I'm spending my time on creative problem solving, using tools that other - often smarter - people made for that purpose.

A knowledge system will not absolve you from thinking. It will free you to spend your time thinking about the right things and at the speed your role now requires.

THE NETWORK SYSTEM

"In a highly networked era, who you know is often more valuable than what you've read."

- REID HOFFMAN, THE ALLIANCE.

Marcel was a good idea that a lot of people made fun of. An AI powered mobile application named for Publicis founder Marcel Bleustein-Blanchet, Marcel was conceived by Publicis executives to solve a network problem. With over thirteen thousand employees, dozens of brands, and offices around the world, Publicis is a sprawling advertising giant. But while it has proprietary data and technology, what makes it formidable is the incredible human talent this mass of creative, technical and marketing employees can bring to bear on behalf of clients.

Back in 2018, for all its brands and organization and offices and people, Publicis relied a surprising amount on word of mouth to connect the right expertise with the right client brief. A client asking to reimagine the shopping journey for cars, how

CRM might transform CPG marketing, or how to advance their challenger brand, would trigger searches of personal networks, agency brands and isolated HR databases. Everyone hearing the call would be left to their own memory, their own experience and their own network to solve that problem.

Marcel was created as an accelerant - to cut across regions, agencies and teams - matching problems and expertise in a few taps of a smartphone.

To say that Marcel was met with hostility is understating it a bit. Tapping into a giant cross agency network for ideas and knowledge cuts against the grain of network agency brands. It runs afoul of trust and culture and relationships that aren't so easily cataloged. Ideas might come from anywhere, but teams prefer to have their own, with others they know and trust. Mixing and matching creatives takes the kind of alchemy you find in bands choosing a lead guitar player or SnL adding new comedians. Chemistry and intangibles often matter more than hard skills.

And that's why the idea of Marcel is too important for any Creative Director to ignore and also too important for you to cede to any individual employer. People are the most important part of your success at this level of the job. Your ability to work with, recruit, grow, hire, deploy, and otherwise engage people will, more than any other thing, decide if you are going to reach your goals. Don't give this up to the people cutting your check.

Develop a system for managing your network. Your extended network. Your goal should be to go far, far beyond the short list of people you know well and trust, and to start collecting and cataloging talent two and three degrees removed. To have a running reference of everyone you have ever worked with, and anyone good you have ever heard endorsed by someone you trust. And I mean everyone. Your system should include every good portfolio that ever passed through your inbox. The name of the funny social media manager for that brand you love on twitter.

The editor at the next table at the award show.

Your memory is not going to be good enough. Neither is the contact list in your phone. Neither is LinkedIn. There's a reason that Salesforce is so popular in large organizations. Having a central place to log and search creatives by skill set will transform how you build and work with teams. As you change jobs, or climb within an organization, and your network grows, it will let you take advantage of the expanse of people you have access to. It will improve your conversations with HR. It will speed up your job searches. It will make you more valuable through what you make available - a reservoir of talent.

Every time I recruit for an open position, our recruiters send me tens and sometimes dozens of portfolios. Instead of choosing a few and moving on with interviews, I take the time to log each one, rate them, tag their skills and add them to my system. I do the same with my own team. And the same with acquaintances, and creatives who pass through my social feeds.

And for all this time and work spent like a rare coin collector of creative talent, I have a large and ever growing database to pull from when a need arises. A set of creatives who, if they aren't available, I can at minimum use to brief recruiting and say "find someone like this." I have a list of people I like working with, and of professional "friends of friends" who come pre-endorsed. In the always changing creative talent market, I have a place to start.

Your network is too important to leave to your employer or LinkedIn. Create your own system. It will be an asset throughout your career.

YOU

BE THE PLAYER'S COACH

"Listen, I know i've been labeled as a player's coach, and I'm proud to wear that badge. But i'll be honest, I think there's a misconception about a player's coach, and that Oh, the players like him - he's their buddy. And my players know this: just because I don't walk around like I have to put fear in their hearts, that doesn't mean the demands aren't going to be extremely high. I've always been a believer that being a coach doesn't mean there has to be some constant level of discomfort for kids to reach their goals. You can be very demanding, and still make people feel good and still make people feel important - as long as they believe that you have their best interest at heart."

- MARCUS FREEMAN, HEAD COACH UNIVERSITY OF NOTRE DAME FOOTBALL

As I write this we are through the Great Resignation and have moved on to Quiet Quitting. Americans, for the first time in my forty four years on this planet, are rethinking our relationship with work. It's overdue. During most of my work life, my European colleagues' favorite comment on American office culture was our pathetic use of our already pathetic vacation allotments. Now almost every interaction I have with London includes the observation that they've returned to office, tucked into the open-ended question of why we haven't. Why we won't.

Oh balance, how good it feels. Give yourself a minute. Luxuriate in it. Then move on to the tricky part - what does leading a creative team mean during a generational change in power dynamics?

Getting the best out of people is a weird balancing act in the best of times. Some combination of open ended and directive. Asking questions and making demands. Structure and space. Managing, coaching, teaching, directing - an exhausting tool set for how to be. And for too many creative leaders the tool of choice is a dickish kind of control.

The aughts gave us popular tech culture, the cult of Steve Jobs and a lot of bad middle managers acting like the assholes who middle-managed them. It's been a twenty year fusing of quality and cruelty in the imagination of work.

But there is no causal relationship. It's possible to make great work with your team without treating them like trash. One has nothing to do with the other.

Getting this right is important in a now-more-than-ever way. In whatever this quiet quitting, resignation refactored time it is we're living in, trying to get great outcomes from control isn't going to work. All things pass. This one for the better. RIP black turtleneck culture.

And the replacement? The mental model I try to use is the player-coach. Being demanding without the power distance. Insisting on progress and quality but communicating without bullying or facetime. Being frank when I know the team is more talented than the work they have made to date, and challenging them to square the two.

It's asking how we can make this better instead of why isn't it. It's leading by example in the unpleasant things - late hours when needed, up-skilling that can seem tedious, doing the boring bits that need doing. It's being socratic whenever possible and directive only when we're out of runway. It's "we did it" wins and "I'm sorry" losses.

Years from now we will mark this as a time of generational change in our relationship with work. A change even more pronounced in high skilled creative fields. For all the hand wringing about the shifts, you can still have nice things, and be a better leader for it.

HUMANITY REQUIRED

"Corporations are people my friend"

\- MITT ROMNEY

t some point in your tenure, the interests of a teammate and the company will diverge.

Don't share that client work in your portfolio - even if you need it to get your next job after we fire you.

You can't say you worked for this name plate agency that will help your career because you really worked for a client specific solution we invented that no one has ever heard of.

It's not in our policy to give bereavement time for the death of a pet so you have to be in for this important presentation, no matter how you feel.

We are going to have to let this person go, the decision has been made, and we're telling you, their manager. We are slow-walking telling them because we have a project we need them to complete and we don't want them to lose motivation.

We're encouraging this person to interview for an internal job to protect ourselves from a lawsuit but truly they have no chance of getting it.

Sometimes these things get said. More often they are understood.

The longer you lead the more you will encounter these situations. There will be incredible pressure, spoken and cultural, to do what the company wants. Sometimes this will put you in a bad place with your own boss, or their boss, or some functionary hiding in the corporate cupboards. They themselves will know the right thing to do is not the thing permitted by the company. They might even try to appeal the decision through the "correct" channels. This is a punt. They know the right thing to do. They know the company forbids it. They are trying to get someone else to make the right decision to avoid responsibility. More often than not, the response will come from HR or a lawyer, and it will quote the party line.

I understand your dilemma, and I have a solution.

Choose the teammate. Break the rule. Deceive management. Don't leave a paper trail. Don't escalate to, or otherwise involve others (an abdication). Do the right thing and make it work.

It will never not be weird to me that this has to be said, but here we are. Corporations are not people. People have hopes, dreams, families, pets, friends, achievements and disappointments. They cry when their feelings are hurt and get mad when they are wronged and stand up for you when you aren't in the room.

Corporations are a paper invention. Like all things born of lawyers, they are artificial and dehumanizing. They are the fake plastic trees of professional life. Bundles of rules and legalese, important only because their authors proclaimed them so.

Not all rules matter and none do all the time. High mindedness about trivial policies is for small minded people - lawyers - not people in the real world. You understand the circumstances. You recognize that this is not a hypothetical trolly problem. You can see this is a decision that impacts the actual wellbeing of an actual person you actually know. You are an adult, responsible for what happens. Don't offload that responsibility to a policy. Don't let a hypothetical confuse you.

I can't tell you what policy it is we're talking about - but I believe you will know it when you see it. Will sense the stupid of it. Choose the teammate. Break the rule.

LEARN TO GARDEN

"The temptation to lead as a chess master, controlling each move of the organization, must give way to an approach as a gardener, enabling rather than directing."

- STANLEY MCCHRYSTAL, TEAM OF TEAMS

C reativity wants a certain amount of chaos. This isn't an army to build. Grip it too tight, over regimen it, and your team will rebel or be reliably boring. A high functioning team and tight control cannot co-exist. The team you want will chafe at your hovering and pointing. Under tight control, the creative muscle atrophies and dies.

But a certain amount of influence is required. If you keep it too loose, if you don't shape it, your team stops being a team at all. Individuals will be good or bad but the parts won't add up to anything. It isn't good enough to hire well, send people a brief and hope for the best. A chef has to taste the soup. A creative director has to see the work. The question is depth and frequency.

This is an art.

Creative leaders under deadline don't want feedback, they want affirmation. Feedback increases stress, late nights and turnover. They start asking where you were two weeks ago when these decisions got made. They calculate the hours of work you're undoing the night before a milestone. They call their significant others and cancel plans. They start losing faith that this is about quality. They suspect you of flexing control. They dig in. They check out.

And yet, you are the one who is on the hook. You are the one accountable if the creative isn't right. If the work isn't good enough you have to say so. Mark and Mary are going to cancel the plans they made two weeks before and you have to tell them sorry, that's the way it is. When that does happen, you are the one that has to enforce quality, but don't confuse that with the way it *should* happen. Your goal is to build a team and culture that knows what good enough is when you aren't there to insist on it. Your goal is never feeling the need to swoop in and save the day because the day does not need saving. Your goal is for Mark and Mary to know what the bar is, and not put you in the position of having to tell them they haven't cleared it.

In his book about modernizing the US Military, Team of Teams, Stanley McChristal describes the leader's role as a gardener. Someone who creates an environment and shapes outcomes without directing individual efforts. He calls this environment "Shared Consciousness" - a team-wide awareness of efforts, successes, failures and direction of travel. This is the kind of control a creative leader should aspire to. You don't make the detailed decisions, you make the environment where good and bad ones are clear.

His plan for reaching this shared consciousness flow state is as simple as it is difficult; over-communication. There is no shortcutting this. If everyone is going to know what quality is and what the values are in a fragmented fast paced and high turnover environment, you are going to have to use as much time and as many tools as you have available to tell them. Team meetings, inspiration channels, work on walls, periodic emails, propaganda, 1:1 skip levels and more, are all chances to reinforce your team values. For as long as you lead, you are in an always-on campaign / listening tour for the minds of the people working with you.

Real control comes from influence. It's about impacting decisions you didn't even know were being made. It's about directing values and culture instead of people. And it's about a lot of gardening on the way.

SAY THE HARD THINGS

"To deal with reality you must first recognize it as such."

- LAURENCE GONZALES, DEEP SURVIVAL

It's impossible to overstate this. So much of leadership is telling people things they don't want to hear.

That idea isn't very good. You weren't representing your work well in that presentation. It's not ok to come in late if you miss meetings to do it. We won't use our award budget to submit this because it has no chance of winning. You can't have that time off because it's right in the middle of the project you asked to be on. We didn't include your concept. You aren't ready to promote (but Natalie is, and into the role you wanted). We put you up for promotion but it wasn't approved. When you leave at five while everyone else on the team is still working to make the deadline, they resent you. You're talking over your teammates. You're talking over your teammates who are women. This idea has been done before, and you should know that. Anthony doesn't want to report to you. Liz doesn't want to work with you. Today is going to be your last day here.

So many things will come to pass if you spend any time leading a team, and it will be your job to communicate them. Many of them will be wrenching, unpleasant conversations. A few won't be as bad as you will imagine beforehand. Some will be much worse. These conversations will never stop. Even with a world beating team, there will be conflict, dissonance, discord and disappointment. Someone must bear the bad news. Someone must hold the banner of unpopular things. Congratulations on your promotion to creative leadership. For the rest of your time here that person is you.

As I got my footing leading teams, I spent a lot of time looking for the "right" answer to the question of how to do this. I read "the Alliance" and the Netflix Culture Manifesto. I read Harvard Business Review's pocket guide for managers and the "Coaching Habit". I read "Radical Candor." While there is a lot of nuanced and thoughtful advice in these texts - I would recommend every one of them - as a whole they take an antiseptic, almost jaunty approach to conversations that often have crushing, if temporary, career consequences. If you are candid about someone's bad performance, and their performance is a thing they care about, you should expect them to be unhappy about it.

But if the alternative is not sharing bad news, or trying to disguise it so it doesn't seem bad, there is no alternative. To be good at this job you need to get accustomed to disappointing people. If that makes you feel bad, it's because you care about people. Hang on to that part. But say the hard things when you have to.

KNOW THE CANON

"You have to know what's been done. And you have to understand it."

           - CORMAC MCCARTHY ON WRITING

Knowing the history of a craft unlocks some intangible things about its nature. Not the worship or backward looking reverence of calcified thinking, but a context. An understanding of how we got here. The lineage of trends and techniques, explored, discarded and recombined makes its own comment on our work in the present.

Great chefs seem to know the lineage of every dish. The discovery of the ingredients. The moment when an approach caught fire. The best coaches in team sports are oral historians of plays, how they emerged, spread through a game and slid from popularity. The new greats remix, reference and break company with the greats who came before. They know when they are standing on the shoulders of giants and when they're jumping off.

There is dishonesty in aspiring to make something new without knowing what was already tried.

Dragging through the history of a thing can seem like a giant waste of time. If someone somewhere thought something about a facet of the craft that we don't even practice today, then so what? This is not a plea that you respect tradition or find a nostalgic streak so much as it is a comment on something that sets the best apart. If you are going to memorize anything in service of being more effective in this job, make it the work. The names of ideas. The fussy details of form factors. The backstory, creative shop and team lead. Remember what was good about it and why. Remember the context where it occurred.

Knowing the canon builds your bar for quality. It lets you recognize if what you are doing now may be lasting in the way that things worth remembering are. It digs a moat against plagiarism and a toolkit for invention. It gives you a vocabulary to use with your team when you have to paint a picture of success or finesse or open revolution. It humbles you.

Know where your own work is in the order of things. Learn the canon of your craft and one day be a part of it.

DESIGN YOURSELF

"No suits. We're not going down there to do their taxes."

- JUDITH CARR-RODRIGUEZ, CEO, FIG

I spent part of my early career at a small creative agency in the SOHO neighborhood of Manhattan. We sat in a maze of interconnected, century-old offices spruced up by an on-staff interior decorator with a love of fake taxidermy. We threw a good party. The vibe was more for-profit co-op than professional agency.

One of my assignments was as part of a team redesigning the website for the National Gallery of Art in Washington DC. The clients were nice enough people who managed to mix the formality of government with the open snobbery of the professional art world. Our cultures were very much not the same.

So it wasn't a huge surprise when late in the project as we prepared for a presentation with their board of directors, one of the account leads let us know they'd received a note asking that we make sure to attend in suits. I was trying to remember if I still owned one when our office president spoke up saying,

"Well, we won't be doing that."

The Account lead tried to argue but she shut him down.

"No suits. We're not going down there to do their taxes. We're us. They're them. No one wears a suit."

End of conversation. It seemed like a strange hill to die on. Our relationship with the clients wasn't even good. In retrospect, she couldn't have been more right.

If you are doing this for money, you report to someone. That someone is looking for you to play a part, and unfortunately, you shouldn't give that someone too much credit. People stereotype leadership in creativity like everything else. They have expectations about you. How you will behave under duress. How likable you will be. Your personal style (Startup? Uniform? Street? Are you going to wear that suit?) and how volatile you will be when pushed. They will note how many visible tattoos you have. These will not have been in the job description or promotion criteria but they are there all the same. For every substantive, results based want, there is an unspoken one searching for vibes.

The creative leaders most in demand are the iconoclasts. The fringe characters who advertise their rough edges. The ones with unmistakable eccentricity. The ones so far out in an extreme position that their peers and business handlers feel duty bound to pull them back. They know when to walk out of a meeting or close (slam?) a door. They're the obsessives. The hard liners. The freaks.

If this sounds petty and childish, that's because it is. This isn't an elevated conversation. There is so little true interest in, or understanding of creativity in professional ranks that you can hardly be surprised by business men and women falling for fancy packaging. Swallow hard, look in the mirror and design a version of yourself that fits the part. And don't wear that suit.

FINANCE IS NOT YOUR PROBLEM

Among the many traps laid for a creative leader to step in, none are quite as insidious as financial responsibility. This might seem like a strange one since rarely are creative leads ever given any financial responsibility at all. What I'm talking about is not the ability to buy a round of drinks on the corporate card. It is a dynamic that shows up in the work at every level when considerate creative leaders account for the demands of other people's positions.

It happens when a PM or Relationship Lead notices the burn rate on the project. You're spending too many hours. That design role needed to get filled by someone more senior to get the look you wanted. The license for the right imagery was more expensive than we intended. This thing is running hot. We can't go back to the client for more money. No way. We're already over. We know you want to do great work, we do too, really. But we're going to need you to pull back a bit. Don't bill so much to this. Use a more junior resource. Wrap it up.

Everything here might be true but it's also not your problem.

Your problem is great work. Your review will be about great work. When your boss decides to promote you or replace you, they will be thinking about if you did great work. They will never ever ever compliment or promote you because your work hit a financial target.

The money, the billing, the margin, the financial headaches are all real. They're also the Relationship Leads problem. Or the Project Managers. Or both. That conversation they had with you to tell you all about them? That was to make those problems yours. It's a good magic trick. Now they don't have to have a conversation with the client asking for more money to do the work they under-scoped. Now they don't have to tell their boss their account isn't going to make margin because of it. Now their problem isn't their problem anymore.

Ignore them and repeat after me - finance is not your problem. In this job, your boss and your boss's boss care about awards, about dazzled clients, about portfolio work, and about any other signal that points to quality. Executive Creative Directors do not care about the finances. When finance does cross your path, it's part of an inherent tension that's built into the system. On one side is the desire for the company to wring as much profit out of a service job as possible. And on the other is the desire for the practitioners of that service to create the highest quality work they can. You're on the second team. Don't ever get confused about that. If you do incredibly profitable work and it's not quality creative, you are only making someone else's bonus bigger. Whatever it costs, however many resources it requires, do whatever you can to make the work great. Damn the finances.

FINANCE IS YOUR PROBLEM

That bit about not needing to know or care? It's true, but it's only half the story. Creative leaders have a well deserved reputation for divorcing ourselves from business reality. We picked this path to be paid for our creativity. Nothing in our education or professional upbringing told us it would lead to spreadsheets. As a result, most creative leaders don't engage with financial details. They duck out of the scope negotiations and glaze over the P&L updates in company town hall. And so as they move up in title, it becomes more and more obvious they are sitting at the kids table instead of where the real decisions are being made.

This is frustrating. Ignorance of the basic underpinnings of the business is disempowering to anyone in a leadership role. Decisions about your team, how many people can be on it, who you can afford to promote and to what level are all taken from you when you ignore the underpinning finances. If someone in another capability tells you we can't afford that, rather than wishing that you could, wouldn't you like to be sure?

Most creative leaders are not sure.

They have no understanding of what roles in what quantity the business can support. They don't know if the training they want to run would mean canceling the holiday party. They don't know what is in the budget for this fiscal year, or even what that is. They don't know and they try not to care. That is no way to use this lever of power.

If you want to be the most effective leader you can possibly be, then finance is your problem. You should know exactly how much you can spend on total salary and ensure that you're spending it in the right roles and on the right individuals. You should know your annual capability budget, and you should spend every dollar of it towards rewards, training, equipment and anything else that's going to make the team better. You should learn how to read a P&L. You should be able to have an argument with anyone in your company about whether you can afford something, with confidence the facts are on your side.

The more senior you are, the more these details are the facts of every conversation. You can't abdicate that to someone else you are hoping has your best interests in mind.

THE CHAOS IS THE GOOD PART

"A sense of humor is not a luxury."

- LAURENCE GONZALES, DEEP SURVIVAL

I have been called into an HR office and told, "I need to show you a security video of some people sneaking onto the roof - where there is a private residence - and see if you can identify them. I think they are on your team." In possibly the clearest security camera footage in the history of the genre, two of my team members trudge past an eye level camera staring straight into it. It had been nice of HR to pretend there was some question of involvement.

I have met a team member at the airport, leaving for a week-long cross country business trip and after noting their lack of luggage, watched their face change to panic as they realized that apart from their laptop, they hadn't brought any.

Two different teammates, years apart, have messaged me from

vacation to ask if they could extend - to insist they had to extend - their trips, because they had met the one. THE ONE. You can't fight love. Both extended. Neither was the one.

An incredible designer at the fulcrum of a difficult project took a brief, said he had it, and then vanished without contact for three terrifying days. The account team melted. I was told we could not reschedule. Plans were made for a "work session" - the classic stall. The designer returned the morning of the presentation, work in hand, clothes dirty, wreaking of smoke and Redbull. The presentation was incredible.

Two teammates were spotted hanging off the back of a New York City garbage truck to get across town after a bar closed in the early hours because they couldn't catch a taxi. Teammates went freelance so they could work around ski season. They demolished all the company furniture in their pod/cube/office and worked on the floor. They set up rogue wireless networks off company hot spots that were faster than company wifi. They used every tool, every account, every forbidden stock library and cloud application.

They went remote van-life but kept on working. They homesteaded through the pandemic and pledged never to return. And never did.

Every year, on the anniversary of when I threw a sandwich at the head of one of my designers, he sends me his version of an "on this day in history" post memorializing my lapse in self control.

I have flown to London for a pitch, canceled seconds after the flight left the gate. Played games to see who could say the word halitosis the most times in a presentation without weirding out the clients. Worked nights and weekends that felt like family vacations. Seen so much fountain swimming at industry functions. Done donuts in rental cars with howling creative partners, doled out high-fives to long lost coworkers on the street in passing with no hello or goodbye.

I have never once wished I was a banker, lawyer or management consultant.

You are lucky to lead this rarest of thing, the professional creative team.

Don't forget to soak in the chaos. It's the good part.

WATER THE PLANTS

"Giving a shit isn't included in the scope but we do it anyway."

- DAVID DROGA

T here are things that are not your job. Are nobody's job. Someone needs to clean up the type styles in the generic deck that the Account team doesn't follow. The small trash can facilities put in the hallway near the bathroom? It is overflowing. Overflows every day by noon at the latest. No one replaces it with a larger one. No one stops using it. If people don't erase the white boards the marker never comes off. The marker is not coming off. Will never come off. Someone wrote "doughnut question - do not erase!" in the top left corner and now no one ever will. The spelling looks wrong but it's the original - shortened in the 1800's. I google it every time we're there, a false start for every meeting in perpetuity. Papers on papers on sketches on post its from a pitch we won four months ago are kicking around one of the huddle tables. We still have those fat plastic desk phones with the gray graphing calculator screens, as if we were going to call someone somewhere in a directory none of us could use with a gun to our head. There's a half inflated cellophane balloon that says "congratulations!" from Amy's celebration toast. It's blowing around the Red-West conference room like an anthropocene tumbleweed, and Amy doesn't work here any more and hasn't for a pretty long time (retirement? forced out? depends who you ask. Good luck Amy). The #PetJokes Slack channel hasn't had a #PetJoke since Labor Day. Hogan the Labradoodle is still sitting there frozen in time from last summer when we were less busy or the pets were funnier or both. It's all just there.

The office plants we asked for - begged for as some humanity in our cold open plan - are dying on the window sills. Snake plants so neglected they no longer thrive on it are calcifying into two foot potato chips. I can't sit near them, even though they have the nice window seats. When I have to work nearby, I face the other way.

Facilities gave us the phones we don't want. We bought the balloons and printed the paper and wrote the writing and told them not throw out the important papers or to erase the writing and we didn't either. I don't even know who the Slack admin is.

It's easier to make than maintain, and a lot more fun.

The neglect will seep into you. The decay and the atrophy will spread and fester until your workplace in all its physical digital everythings are a corporate Grey Gardens. No one will say it quite this way, but it will be very, very sad.

It's your team. You die on this hill.

Water the plants.

HELP THE TEAM.
LEAVE A REVIEW.

Reviews are the only way people hear about this book and every one of them helps. Drop some stars on Amazon or Goodreads. If you have a minute more, let others know what you you fould helpful and what was missing in an honest review.

If there's anything else you want to comment on or argue about, you can find me on Threads (for as long as that lasts) at @andrew.crlsn. I would love to hear from you.

ACKNOWLEDGEMENTS

I have been fortunate to work for some incredible creative leaders. The support, mentorship, and patience they showed me made every difference in my career.

With gratitude, thank you.

- Consuelo Ruybal
- Damian Hasse
- Stewart Katz
- Elliot Kravitz
- Lincoln Bjorkman
- Kip Voytek
- Emil Lanne
- Cedric Devit
- Kim Bartkowski
- Chia Chen
- Atit Shah
- Ronald Ng
- Scott Donaton
- Cathy Butler

ABOUT THE AUTHOR

Andrew Carlson

As a leader of creative teams, Andrew has spent his career building resilient brands through digital transformation and modern marketing. Throughout, his focus has been developing novel solutions to complex problems involving design, technology and culture. His passions include team development, organizational optimization, and new business. He has helped create experiences for BlackRock Financial, National Instruments, Whole Foods, American Express, Goodyear, CVS, Stoli, and Taco Bell.

His work has received top industry honors, been featured in FastCompany and CommArts and he has served on award juries for The ONE Show and Effy Awards, as a jury Chair for the AIGA awards and has been featured by Ad Week as a Mobile Innovator.

Andrew lives in California with his wife and human-sized dog.

Printed in Great Britain
by Amazon

27455499R00086